CW01666187

Crannóg 62 sprin

ISSN 1649-4865
ISBN 978-1-907017-72-8

Cover image: *Growth* by Blake McGrane-Corrigan
Cover design by Wordsonthestreet
Published by Wordsonthestreet for Crannóg magazine @CrannogM
www.wordsonthestreet.com @wordsstreet

Crannóg is proudly
supported by Galway City Arts Office.

Faigheann Crannóg
tacaíocht ó Oifig Ealaíon na Gaillimhe.

the arts council an chomhairle ealaíon
funding literature artscouncil.ie
Comhairle Cathrach na Gaillimhe
Galway City Council

CONTENTS

Submissions for Crannóg 63 open May 1st until May 31st
Publication date is September 26th 2025

Crannóg is published bi-annually in spring and autumn.

Submission Times:
Month of November for spring/summer issue.
Month of May for autumn/winter issue.

We will not read submissions sent outside these times.

POETRY:
Send no more than three poems. Each poem should be under 50 lines.
PROSE: Send one story. Stories should be under 2,000 words.

We do not accept postal submissions.
When emailing your submission we require three things:

1. *The text of your submission as a Word attachment.*
2. *A brief bio in the third person.*
3. *A postal address for contributor's copy in the event of publication.*

For full submission details, to learn more about Crannóg magazine, to purchase copies of the current issue or take out a subscription, log on to our website or scan the code:

www.crannogmagazine.com

This issue of Crannóg is dedicated to
the memory of

Maeve Joyce-Crehan
1961 – 2025

Maeve passed away on 16th of January 2025.

Suaimhneas síoraí dí

The Crannóg Bursary

The Crannóg Bursary is awarded to one contributor to each issue of *Crannóg*.

When each contributor to *Crannóg* is accepted for inclusion in the magazine they are invited to make a short, simple application for the Crannóg Bursary.

The bursary amounts to €1,500 per issue and the recipient is announced on our social media platforms.

We are grateful to writer Marian Kilcoyne for her sponsorship of the Crannóg Bursary.

my tbr is neverending

Laura Theis

tonight I'm reading
the sky again

looking for clues
amongst its vivid

birds I'm reading
the shadows

that surround
each small but brilliant

source of light
I am reading a million

protest signs composed
of petals

they can take away
the books

but the story
still moves forwards

they cannot steal
the story's ending

when its teller is
the world

A Darling Waste Of Time

Patrick Deeley

The trees, said by a different clock
to the one I attend,
bring me round.

Their words to each other happen
slowly as the mycelial
web-works pass between them.

I listen, hear nothing,
but this is my darling
waste of time. Paths, pawprints,

ramshackle rose bushes
trembling along the quarry lane,
a tiny flower

sprouting out of the shell
of an old lawnmower.
And here, a beetle in a rain barrel

running rings,
the glint of sand
becoming an ant, sun-quickened.

Notes for my surf instructor (or, How I want to love)

Ana Reisens

I want to learn how to fall. Spectacularly
and with no room for doubt. These hands,
these feet – let them be made for everything

I cannot keep, everything we were never meant
to hold. Let me be bold. Breathless. Simple.
Let me become a smith to the sea foam, an anvil

to the sand. Let the white gulls spin above me,
chuckling, the minnows kiss my puckered skin.
Let me laugh, sputter, laugh again, become dizzy.

Then let me sit, become whole, become certain.
The clouds, a curtain. This body. Let the water rise
and fall, the wind pull at its eternity.

Let me be this.

In the Woods the Mosses Speak to the Trees

Dolores Walshe

Remember when our giraffes the far side
of our oceans ate all our first acacias?

How before they died the trees warned
their kin further afield and their kin

sent bitterness into their leaves to save them
selves? Regrettably none of your signals

ahead can arrest the coming slaughter.
Today will bring alarm, plunder, disarray,

this will be your last sunrise, already sounds
of rumblings in the ground, the scent of diesel

has driven our creatures to flee, seek shelter
in your young lining the ridges above us.

This is an old story and it is hard. You
will lose your lives to new roofs or a set

of stairs, a bowl hewn to hold fruit or an
admiring gaze, coffins to house their dead.

You will learn the language of muteness,
the art of stillness, you will live with us

in the memory of what you once were, know
only the purpose your lives were taken for.

We grieve with you too knowing we can do no
more for you, heading as we are into dormancy.

But this is a skill we excel in, a lesson learnt
over aeons. We will desiccate in the sun's rays

wait for the rains to revive us, do what we can
to keep all together until we can re-group

once more, stabilise that which is unstable,
alter temperatures, break rock, build soil,

re-house our insects, anchor our plants,
nurture our young. Remember, remember

we are everywhere, in cracks in their pavements,
roofs, walls, their ornamental garden rockeries,

deeper still in their folk memory when our bread
fed them in times of fever and want. Take heart.

Remember there are small pockets of resistance
everywhere, a growing movement that offers

us light, the gift of our gift. Remember wind
floodwater fire, they too will teach the inevitable.

Remember how we begin again again agai ...

Place du Panthéon, 1919

Linda Ibbotson

Inspired by The Magnetic Fields – a surreal poem written in 1919 at Hotel des Grands Hommes by André Breton and Philippe Soupault.

As the city awakens, I listen to the music of the street –
the garbage trucks, the conversation of birds,
the cry of the hawker selling goats milk, the lone violin
and I want to touch every note.

From my balcony, I look across *Place du Panthéon*
to the statue of a philosopher.
My thoughts fragment like grey clouds around the neck of Rousseau,
as if ruins of a dark winter.
At his feet, a shadow, cut in the shape of a cross
reminds us of the ultimate betrayal.
Nearby, white doves devour yesterday's bread and fish.

His gaze follows the soft curve of La B*ibliothèque Sainte-Geneviève*,
its neoclassical façade containing history's pen –
ancient scripts written on mulberry bark,
now resembling fragile paper wings.
Dead names carved into flesh.

In the asylum there are remnants of war.
The sound of rifles still ricochet in half-limbed ears,
ripening fruit of almond trees fall like bullets
into rivulets of blood, the colour of night.
Heroes howl as if a chorus of ravenous wolves.

In the thin morning air, the *Panthéon* shimmers,
as if a surreal hub of a Phoenician ship,
its captives of scholars and revolutionaries
bound where silent walls begin.
At the portico, Corinthian columns
resemble teeth of a great white shark,
seeking to devour.

I long to turn away from the lament of death,
the things left at the altar of ruins,
to spread ashes in the place light is beginning to open,
to write, until nothing else matters.

On the History of the Great Plains

Ciarán O'Rourke

Black Elk, 1863 – 1950

I remember after everything, older than before,
in loneliness, the both of them heart-weary
as they drew their son away, the disenchanted
visionary, a still-ebullient boy at heart,
his wounded carcass draping now
across a pony-drag two nodding horses towed:
our mutilated prophet, his parents' single child,
dispatched. I can see him living clearly
in my mind. When the storm of vision drops
like this, and lifts again, the murdered world itself,
for all our grief, seems greener: the spring
of second sight unfolding cleanly, like a rain.
Later, the famed, unflinching service-men –
you know their kind – came with carnage
on a winter's day, the weather fresh,
a deep sun shining out, as they hunted
through the valley, humming songs.
We fought them, flailing in the volleys
as we fell. The wind rose after, dreaming night,

a deathly blizzard forming in its wake: the snow-drifts
whispered through the gully, gathering in banks
around the crooked heaps of children broken down
by bullets as they ran; the women, too, ripped through
and going grey, their butchered bodies hillocks in the snow.
Mark it down, but also that the vision carries on.
It's in the cloudiness of sight alone
we stumble from the way. All – vividly collected
or brutally effaced – is vision, only vision, in the end.

Lafcadio's Wife

Tracy Gaughan

In Japan, fathers are trees, mothers snow.
A narrow road is never gone alone.
This morning, trees can see their souls
in the lake, fathers meet their sons in the
shadowed mass, a discoloured iris. I
remember how myopia brought you
closer to Kokoro, the heart of all
that matters. Your pocket telescope for
the silk crop on our distant winding hill,
a magnifying glass for the woodcuts
and camellias – vestigial.
Lafcadio, my little no-one son,
and forebear of yourself, your spirit rests
like mist on the water, and the moon I
know is you, is a fish caught in golden
bulrush. I loosen a memory caked
in coarse salt and grilled over the fire
in the Cherry Garden, the hot meat
burns Kazuo's fingers and you kiss them
cool as shade. A wood duck takes my arrows
of love across the silent pond and when
a zephyr whips the beech leaves up like
Monarchs awake at last, I feel you in

the air. No-one son, how you ached to
understand the yurei-daki's motives,
why the young women playing shamisen
sang in their sleep The Flowers of Edo.
Why the cuckoo tempted a poet in
Kyoto. How I wove your tender sail.
A storyteller of moonlight and rain,
you took with you your travelling diary,
by a force of karma glimpsed the core of
my country. Sensed its essence, kept it safe
as a stone inside the peach of your mind.
No-one son, father of history.

Mirroring Me

Martina Dalton

---

against the sky, a curlew releases
liquid shrieks of barely manageable grief.
A group of sweetling birds rise up, then quickly fall
like a deck of cards to a croupier's waiting hand.

A stonechat finds the most unlikely branch
to bear his weight.
Two young lovers who do not yet know
they will settle here for life, dangle their feet

look out to sea, fingers meeting briefly,
where the skin of sky meets earth.
Now that summer's tent has packed its anchor poles,
the circus ponies' prints begin to sprout

as if by magic,
bright green shoots – sea lavender and samphire.
Each evening the torn places fill, are soothed
by the water's silk. Slow as if it's the first time,

coming in. Silver leaves from yesterday's storm
form the basis of a nest.
Along the narrow path that joins the land to sea
the midden dross presents itself.

A shrew, new to death, begins to disappear
where it's been dropped – or left it late to feed.
Each night depending on her day, how overwhelmed
she's been, sea lays her rockweed hem:

sun bleached crabs, matted with the feather-bones
of dead sea birds. She kicks it along the base of the bank;
drops her seaweed clothes –
heavy as wet hair.

On Lindow Moss

Elizabeth Barton

In 'The Life and Death of a Druid Prince', Celtic History scholar Anne Ross and archeological chemist Don Robins hypothesise that Lindow Man was a druid sacrificed to the Celtic gods in an attempt to halt the Roman offensive after Boudica's defeat in AD 60.

They came for us on the sixth night of the moon.
No fires blazed on the hilltops as they rounded us up,

led us to a forest clearing. When we drew lots, I knew
the charred piece of barley cake would fall to me –

I was the youngest, fresh from druid school, mysteries
dancing on my tongue. As I knelt down, not yet ready

for the thunderblows, the priests chanting over me,
I pictured my dead father, felt his embrace as the axe

split my skull. I slumped to earth but they killed me
again and again. They drained me of lifeblood,

carried me through whispering pines to the place
of rushes and dark water. The birch leaves shivered

as they laid me face down in the pool. The mire
nestled me in moss, cradled me in her womb of peat.

For centuries, I've been resting here but if my body
should rise from the bog and you see my bones

restored to oak, my skin to lichen, may my wounds
be a whistle warning you that the iron wheel

keeps on turning, that in times of terror, you'll rush
to sacrifice your young, your wise, over and over.

The Wild Hedge and the Cut Hedge

Winifred McNulty

I'm all roots, slashed branches.
I knew you before, you couldn't be contained
Scratched tractors, berries for kids, shelter on windy nights
or howling. I was dark sky sculpture.
You put it up to the ESB
We called it 'crossing the line'
You were a conjurer, a wizard, a shape shifter
Didn't know my own strength, the birds saved me for a while.
How so?
The jay was here, blue tits, there were boxes wedged under my oxters.
And then
Crab apple blossom in spring like confetti.
I was so jealous
In Storm Dennis, crews, all day climbing, sizing me up, even
a fella from the council, in the middle of the road, eyeing me up and
down
We never imagined you'd be the first
See where the old beech sprang out of me, see the nails
from one of Parnell's posters, I grew round them.
That day he came with the splicer, gleaming, sinister

I could take the nails, the children swinging out of me, the lovers
sheltering,
I set the road glimmering with shadows I cast.
It's coming to us all
Frost nights its raw, cold to the marrow.
Throw us a few leaves.

Leave Well Enough Alone

Finola Cahill

My mind feels like the top
press with the good delph, or a dead
person's closet. I keep picking

up things I shouldn't – the fox fur,
the butter dish. Checking smell,
texture. The egg cup with the painted

violet. It is like sinking – powdery
velvet boots, Christmas lights,
novelty cat cake stand. I palm

the past and weigh it against
my car keys, the pint of milk. Time
eats itself. Ironed shirts, still hung.

You, speaking, lips shrugging my throat – almost
a locked drawer, almost a cracked dinner plate.

Heaney & Me

Ger Duffy

He takes me to Toner's bog, I follow him
to where the body was found – bones, partial skin,
kidneys and toenails intact since 500 BC. He points
out bog cotton, bog violet, rare orchids, bog bean, bog

myrtle, bog asphodel, a Siberian crane – it is *all*
so interesting! He hands me a tin can, we pick *fraocháin**,
fewer than previous years, he sighs. A bush creaks
in the wind, he holds my hand as he helps me over a ditch,

I am walking on air. He has found a cache of bog butter,
to have with the scones his aunt has made for us
and a HP bottle of warm tea, *corked sloppily with paper.*
I think of a *goose's wing* on the floured board,

the sunlit yard, her whitened nails. I have him all to myself
as we sit on a Foxford rug, surrounded by *black butter soil,*
flat as far as the eye can see, sunlight trains down on us
steady as a gun. His shoulders *globe like a full sail*

as he stretches his legs, his crumpled suit shiny at the knees,
his hair frothy as hawthorn. I cannot think of what to say,
I ask him why he never tried surrealism. He smiles,
Sure, what could be more surreal than this?

**Fraocháin – bilberries.*

Whistle

Elizabeth Gibson

You see tin whistle I've been having feelings
about you blue-silver-sky notes
they say my-soul-as-my-instrument poems are done
to death but you are not my soul are you?
You are at least my fourth instrument I am hardly fluent
but I know your mechanics more *naturally*
than the key-things drum-things string-things
that *are* me large-bodied led by hands
using my voice-place is a new country
I go from horse to barn owl peering into the life
of the flute-oboe-clarinet people
that I never was at school they had such pretty names
is it a coincidence I found you
the year I grew taller and stiller through a cormorant
found faith in turquoise note of kingfisher
cascading over river my arm was cut open
after my palm went numb my two little fingers

I can spare exactly   two   fingers on a whistle
leaving six   to dance across   the holes
tease out the birdcall I heard at the quarry never placed
I trust myself now to store it   forever in my fingers
though it doesn't seem to exist
maybe I heard myself   calling back through time
to the person terrified   of impending surgery
maybe Mam heard me   fifty years ago in her father
and brother   non-stop whistling filling the house
Dawning of the Day? she asks   and hey whistle
we manage   I never thought I could   be this.

Easter 2024

Kevin Graham

Earlier we stood in Croke Park and turned as a collective
towards the flag, its spark, the band's imperative
sounding out the anthem before the throw in.
I turned fifteen again, singing *Amhrán na bhFiann*
without knowing its meaning on the basketball court
of a summer Gaeltacht. *Irish men and Irish women ...*
boys and girls, really, hormones flying through
the bloodstream cruelly, afraid what we might do
in the light of the *rince* when the sun lowered
to catch the burning ochre in the eyes of a belovèd.

Are deference and weight allusions to politics?
If only they knew the like the system would inherit:
shapeless junkies hooked on power ballads,
crooning to the masses for a few limp votes.
Earlier the President lay a wreath and observed
a minute's silence, the sky's unseemly blue streaked
with contrails from the Air Corps whose direction
couldn't be questioned. Difficult to not despair
when terms like 'brilliant', 'brave' and 'courageous'
are as far as you can get from the civic bourgeoisie.
'Cowardice' and 'rapine' are the trending topics,
one's public persona a woven crown of thorns.

Speaking of terrible beauty, the Royal Canal sports
traffic cones and rat-borne disease. I know this felicity
may seem a little OTT but, noticing the towpaths
shut with ugly fencing, it's valid to scratch
one's head and wonder where it's all going.
Days we'd spend in summer with our nerves jangling
along the banks, waiting for love to come and tap us
on the shoulder. The song plays on, its impetus
hanging at the centre of our being where wings
meet a metal gate, their blur a clarion call for living.

Leaning over a glass cabinet in Trinity College Dublin,
those dead generations come back to ghost
the shadows looking down: tourists lined up in droves
to understand the frown frozen in their brows.
Future's lost trajectory is a library steeped in history
so it can be grasped that under her manhood
were British army posters recruiting Irish volunteers.
An enquiry from the front. The gall. Who plucked
the sniper bullet from the wall of knowledge?
That supreme hour felt and unfettered, its pledge
unable to be lost, the children of the nation
still waiting to learn that April could be august.

In island light, the room

Katherine Duffy

becomes a gallery, its careful squares
filled with the wild

performance art of gulls,
a tiny ship on a faraway line.

Bric-a-brac of stones and shells,
loot from long windy walks,

the little green crab you found the other day,
its body a casket, bearing a mark

like a keyhole. Decisions,
those challenging pieces,

make their presence felt,
brutal in their simplicity.

Light a fire, lace up your boots.
Leave or stay. Then again

you could just linger a while, here at the table,
the table with its hasty flowers,

its loving old chairs. Take
your place at the centre, let

the light fall, distance play
havoc with your bones.

Missteps of hills and hunger

Fatema Alzari

watermelon on a roof
of palm and stone
you hide from your father
who brings a broom
to your back
as you spat the seeds
barely restraining
the juice on your chin
from leaving a mark
   you told me once
on the way to mekkah for hajj
the bus broke down
like knees to the earth
twenty women
prayed to the cracked skin
of the desert stars
each constellation, a map
you unspooled for no return
   fathers, brothers, husbands
already arrived in mekkah
dressed in their ihram:
two pieces of white fabric without stitching
as the night air cradles
your bare foot, licks
the dune of your shoulders
your voice swells to perfume
and you confess
you stole a piece of the ihram
for your real pilgrimage
where you walked for three days
hoping to get as far as possible
from sewing back the other half

Portrait of a Lakeland Hare

Ruth Gilchrist

The artist has understood where you sit
the grass bent silver side up,
knows the depressions where you half rest
to wipe the news from your whiskers.

Before the day's last industry
lays copper threads across your shoulders
she comes, again, to interpret.

As she smits and smudges your nose
do you taste the salt on her fingertips?
When your coal tipped ears sweep the sky
do you hear her dreams become graphite?

As she catches the last dash
of a golden day and hangs
it in your eye, do you recognise her?

My Mother at the Sink

Catherine Balaq

Some days I slip out into the garden.
I wait there until it gets dark and I eat
soil in handfuls, thick fresh loam
like the earth I remember my mother
scraping from new potatoes.
Up to her elbows at the sink
sleeves rolled, mud under her nails
and her wedding ring, telling me
how she scrubbed vegetable peelings
from hotel bins to feed her sisters.
And I cry while I eat soil, sat under
the lime trees waiting for kindness
to engulf me, to wash me clean of sin,
to wash the shame of this from my skin.

From the New World

Barbara Dunne

After Dvořák

Somewhere, there are musicians
playing a violin sonata. Notes float
among the trees and shrubs. While I pull
and tug deep rooted weeds. Unlucky
to be flourishing in this patch of ground
I now call home. With clay clod hands
I exume these dandelions and thistles.
With tender feet I step among the flowers.
For who knows when the day will come
when I will be plucked from this earth.
Wrapped like a spring bulb and nestled
into the cold earth, to the strains
of 'Largo', from Symphony No. 9.

High Tea

Annie Egan

If not now then when precisely
is the right time
to drink mushroom tea?
When finishing touches
have been applied with love to wise children
and sweet grass comforts the garden
When worth is cut adrift from productivity
the far horizons draw close
and we strive no more
When I've danced my last
on the pelvic floor
lights dimmed and steps forgotten
With thickened soul and fissured skin
teeth set free
this grip well softened
I will look to the stars long gone
from the warm face
of an unmade bed
Count my ducks
with all their blessings
then let them go
and boil the kettle.

Free Gaff

Rebecca D'Arcy

Summer, 1997

You sat at the table drinking tea
while we knocked back cans of Dutch Gold.
It took my breath away to see your bones,
the inside of you, so bare.
Some savage knife had pared you down,
spared no inch of the girl I had known.

Later I spoke to your brother
who said you weighed out your food,
made tiny piles of raisins,
sucked on a sweet and spat it out.
Those were your rituals,
that was your way.

And we thought we were doing so much better,
with our eyeliner, smokes and cans,
worshipping lads in bands,
watching our boyfriends play Final Fantasy on the PlayStation.
Sidelining ourselves,
that was our way.

On cold nights

Bern Butler

our mother pinioned us with blankets
scratchy close-woven yellowed with dreams
secured them with pins like you'd see on a kilt
could have pushed us from shore in the cot
and we would not have fallen out even
if we wrestled in the night our bodies
were cubs roots soft limbs entwined
below the low-roofed set in sleep
our senses commingled smells the arm
flung across my face was a sail,
shutter come loose in the wind branch
tapping the window in the book
I was reading woman weeping in the attic
when I woke my sister's hair
splayed across the pillow
was the blue-black wing of a raven
she was older soon off on her travels
and though we woke on the other side
of night to the same bright yellow room
no small thing was shifting

Triptych

Theodore Deppe

1

Is it really half a century
since the sky above Davis Hollow
pulsed with almost continuous lightning,

drawing me out into the Kentucky night
to see if a funnel cloud was forming?
By morning, over a hundred twisters

escorted death into nearby towns
whose names read like battlefields:
Xenia, Brandenburg, Monticello.

2

If I were a painter, I'd render
all those fatalities in one panel, then sketch in
the beginning of new life in the next,

a few weeks later in Davis Hollow
when lightning bugs entered
through open windows and circled

the bedroom. I'd borrow the golds
of Gabriel's wings in da Vinci's Annunciation
and let everything glow, everything swirl.

3

And now our daughter calls from Asheville
to tell us in her fiftieth year she's found
the Fountain of Youth. At their gathering

last night, everyone became children,
catching tree frogs and pollywogs,
catching lightning bugs. I still have no idea

if time is a burning wheel or just a slight tip
forward, but in Cait's account of the party,
the tree frogs of her childhood sang all night.

If Time Could Fly

Áine Rose Connell

Who else could have warmed this heart of mine?
Those days, we let love push our life's plans

into tight bedsits, warm balmy evenings,
laughing, the odd shared cigarette.

If time could fly away like a swallow
and not hurry back to where it all began.

There was never any rush on us.
There is never any rush on love.

Who else could have tested the laws of time,
defied the cynics' plight, found me no longer

singular, but unified, tied
like a ribbon to you, this gift, this husband of mine.

This upright-turned rugby collar turned down.
A lot of our years together like bird flight;

I was a wren fleeting in the multicultural bath of East London,
you that old barn owl, holding me up like the blue dim belly

of Ealing Twilight, never swaying from pinpricking skyline.
In less glamorous years, I plucked broccoli from the soil

in South Western Australia, the Carnaby to your cockatoo.
When we headed east to Sydney, to Chinese tea gardens,

it was not necessarily tea that was drunk but cold pints
in glasses, clinking together under butcher pink sunsets

we cheers'ed to all of this, to all our life.

Meadows

Patrick Moran

In me still, those childhood meadows
which fostered sorrel, yellow rattle,

tufted vetch and clover;
which were sanctuaries

for nesting corncrakes and skylarks;
whose swaths I used to turn

with a rhythmic nudge of prongs,
and raise to dome-like trams ...

Now, glutted with boosters,
deflowered, devoid of birds,

I quiver in the teeth of blades,
am sucked into giant maws ...

I shrink into plastic wrapping.
I ooze out of silage pits.

This is the poem in which I left you

Janice Warman

This is the poem in which I am still alive.
This is the poem in which I left you,
the white gate clicked softly shut behind me,
the yew tree hung low over the driveway,
and your dog came running: 'Jump in,' I said,
and opened the door. The cat in her basket

on the back seat trilled a welcome,
the car hummed over the speed bumps,
the horses in their field whickered to each other.
She's leaving, she's leaving, she's leaving,
they said quietly. My horse was already gone,
already unloaded from a clean trailer

and led into a clean stable. Safe. Nobody
dragged me back through the gate,
nobody cracked my head between the
door and the jamb, it is the poem in which I had
already started the car and driven away.
It is the poem in which I am still alive.

Foreign Study

Annie Deppe

Who was she? Fifty years later
I remember travelling back across London to Crouch End
and Mrs Catania's rented rooms. It was evening
as the bus vibrated to a stop at the edge of a park
to let a young woman slowly descend.
Her pale face was lit by neon. Rain
darkened her hair. A thin coat pulled tight
against the damp. Beneath her arm,
a large art portfolio.

Earlier, the professor of my drama course
propositioned me in the hall
as the other students waited beyond closed doors.
He was in his forties with a florid face
and even as I turned him down
I wondered if I would still pass his class?
'How inappropriate' he said of my plan
to hike the Isle of Skye with my boyfriend.

The bus rumbled to life as the young woman
stepped back and then walked away into the night.
She was limping. And already it was too late
to follow her. Or, for reasons I'm trying tonight
to understand, to forget her.
To the Lighthouse lay in my lap, just begun.
Her departure something like a strong red line
down the middle of a page.

Small Talk

Gerard Smyth

---

for Pauline

At night we talk about the day.
The small catastrophes,
what we let slip through our hands.
And if the day was uneventful
we talk about something else – a book
that won't let us forget its pages of suspense.
You might tell me I am out of touch
because I can't understand the fuss
about Taylor Swift, why all the kids love her.
It's never a long conversation,
sometimes no more than a question and answer.
We might disagree on which of us
asked the other to dance
or the number of days we were snowbound
because our first house was on high ground.
Or you might recall a Sunday drive
to go blackberry-picking on the banks
of the Boyne, a holiday taking our ease
on the sands of Rossnowlagh

or maybe that evening we had the Danube
to ourselves or so it seemed in Budapest.
After making love you led the way,
more by intuition than reading the map –
down to the river where the water was calm,
the fireflies phosphorescent in the dark.

Winter Painting

Maria Isakova Bennett

After he left, I spent months tracing moves
of artists I love – smears of blue and red,
of blood, of fallen fruits. As days lengthened

and shortened, I became content
with the play between brush and canvas –
Impressions moved through me: some

from my past – the short life of pears for my father,
for the men I've loved; some from the table –
vermillion cloth to welcome winter, to make it hot.

Awake and asleep, I try to read a message. Words
will not remain still. I capture (say) berries, wine,
or bowl, place them on the cloth, offer them as petition.

Garrus

Billy Fenton

A curve of rocks
divides the bay –

Manannán's teeth,
blackened and broken,

crack
into the Underworld.

We take
to the water,

near the place
where I cut

your hair,
wiry strands

washed over
by breaking waves.

Two choughs
glide past,

silky black,
red beak & legs

like fresh sparks
in the ashes.

The Bus

Bill Richardson

This bus travels only one direction,
past damp grass arrayed with sheep and lambs.
And what he wants to know, when I get home,
is whether it was very crowded.
I haven't seen him in eleven months
though my dreams contain him often,
as the fields I pass contain a world we share
and find it hard to speak.

Small mountains flee before my thoughts,
like when we crossed a soggy field
to reach the tree we'd christened Jacob's Ladder.
He'd lifted all my lightness
and lodged my ten-year bones
on that knotted branch where I could start my climb
as silence swelled between us.

The lambs admired by mothers in the field,
the ewes who cannot share a dream,
what do they know of country lanes and buses?
Oh, what things he might have told me
when my children came along,
but legacy's a one-way street.

Dad, the bus was almost empty.

[so, from a point of being here]

Ray Malone

'my own hand has long since taken flight in writing'
— Michel Serres, *The Five Senses*

so, from a point of being here, perched to pretend again,
that, after all, flight might be possible, with the aid of words
and the wind that lifts them from the page, when it stirs,
or the memory of that first music, raising everything up
from the dust, forcing its way through to the core,
to the source of all, the body born to breathe, the limbs
to be lithe, the feet themselves to find their rhythm, here,
to found their own inimitable dance, step by step, sound
by sound, to the blood's tune drumming in the mind, trembling
at the mere touch of the earth's otherness, from tenderness
to the turning rage, from turbulence to the least leaf:
poised, between the to and fro of forms, the rise
and fall of days, the impossible dreams beyond mere sleep,
and the waking, weighed with the freight of what's to be done.
what to be gone, what to come, what world to fly to,
what from, what music to make of the way, the meanwhile
of waiting, walking on, the if and when of where to pause:
and why not here:
there is no height, of either day or night, from which to fly,
but perhaps a place to be, as if forever, on the point of

Infected

Wendy Mooney

Things were simpler then –
the street-facing window a portal to a world without me in it,
whiff of bleach from the kitchen,
the duvet draped over my knees with the door flung
open to the washing-line –
baubled clothes floating –
the illness taking me nowhere in particular,
once accepted, gracious –

until the rains came, great lines of latitude on our pond
that set the goldfish jumping;
damp sheets at night on the rickety bed
a ticket to hallucinations,
spirits of the race track, unanticipated guests:

a shopkeeper unrolling waves of fabric
behind a wooden counter above my head;
a lover from the future found amongst the ice floes
still alive – his intuitive eyes –
the daytime all confused with the night;
the hiss of rain an ever-present sound;
soup held to my lips again when things were going good.

The traffic slow on George's Street outside.
The frogs abandoning the pond –
bog-red in the kitchen, weed-clad in the stopped drain.
The ever-present hiss of rain.

His eyes.

petty king

Arlene Pattison

before they dug him out they said a prayer
above the tangled wreath of root and gut
and soft red fronds that might have been his hair
or lichen running through his throat's short cut
in seams of silt and ancient sills of schist
below the bridal sway of cotton froth
three small blue beads inside his leather fist
the old king rises wrapped in peat-brown cloth
his wedding night still stains his mouth like wine
a wild-eyed forfeit offered up to pay
for fly agaric dreams of the divine
we do not know how lonely long he lay
halfway between believing and belief
the bog lies like a lover through his teeth

157

John Saul

The decibels, the dust. The trauma. Low on a universal scale – far, far below the level of slavery, the Dust Bowl, the *Titanic* – but a trauma. The horror story responsible is the brainchild of the Browns next door: the bone-pounding construction of a monumental rear extension. A botoxed house. Did I say brainchild? What brain? But a trauma. Birdsong is being replaced by pile-drivers and jackhammers, sunlight with cement dust. As the walls rise up to form the monstrosity, flakes of stone and concrete zing from electric saws, and when all is done, on top will come the final indignity, a stupid twirling weathervane. But now at any moment, more pounding, pounding. Freaking me out.

I'm new to traumas, but I could weep, and I have. Now that the tears have dried and I'm well into the aftermath, I aim to come out fighting. In this account of the annihilation of neighbourly peace I want depth, humanity. I want the tale to be told with weight like the Bible, yet light as air, fresh and cool like aquamarine. The word *universe* should feature, its roar be heard.

Everyone involved has been such a disappointment. The Browns, I choke at the thought of them – goodness, what a let-down. The council officers too, the architects, the inspectors, such disappointments. The result? Added together, these wretched instances of humanity drove me down, down, into the depths. From there I did the unexpected.

I bought a surveyor fish.

I gave it a tank to swim in. With warm waters, gently lit and aerated, day and night. It was clearly of a noble species, with its fiery red trunk and feathery black fins in fine combed lines. Overwhelmed by the glory of this creation, I took a while to see past the dazzle. But, as if guessing something was up, the fish had from the beginning a startled look. I looked into its history. Its forebears started out in north-east Mexico, and now this offspring found itself in cold and clammy latitudes; that may have had something to do with that alarmed expression, the constant darts and flicks about the tank. That's enough about the fish. As usual I could hardly hear myself think. The tank vibrated as the Browns' builders bored and thundered into the murderously hard ground, excavating great pits for the foundations to their brainless monstrous fuck-you rear extension. Fuck you is not quite accurate. *Everyone* in hearing was fucked. Even the animals. Does a fish hear a pneumatic drill? (It's one of those questions. Do birds have tongues?)

The tank developed a leak. The water seeped out. I'd been gone hours, giving my ears and bones a day off. The noble fish lay still on a wet rock. I wanted the neighbours to also lie on wet rocks. They deserved wet rocks. I wanted them to lie gasping and die.

I was about to give the surveyor fish a name, Danny, but hesitated. It was a name he would never know.

Aptly, at this time of earth-shaking bombardment, an innocent creature lying there, wet but lifeless, I was reading B.S. Johnson's account of a medieval cathedral about to be shelled to smithereens. In his account the work and skills of scores of artisans, centuries of construction, are destroyed in seconds.

I am indebted to B.S. Johnson, undeniably, but to be effective my account needs the opposite of long construction and instant destruction. I want the trauma of drawn-out destruction, culminating in the passing away of a fish so innocent, to be followed somehow by swift delight, joy, by whatever means. If not joy then retribution, for having such shitty neighbours. O god of retribution, make them become so bloated they burst. Have them nuked, hit by a drone strike. The house explodes, implodes? I want a new neighbour. A neighbourly soul, who brings no trauma, no hammers, grinders or compressors, only apricot trees and golden wheat and greenery. I have Linda in mind, a certain Linda.

After all you and your forebears have been through, Danny, if you only knew what did for you. It was a bombastic juddering fuck-fish rear extension.

Before the first concrete-breaking jackhammers had arrived the Browns' project had already spouted: 109 e-mails, 4 architects' plans, 3 sets of comments to the council, 4 council decisions, 1 15-page University of Salford article on the impartiality of party wall inspectors, 4 articles on appeals, 22 people contacted for professional advice, 8 visits to the property, 1 24-page final plan, the figures on its drawings only legible in bright light by magnifying glass (special purchase), countless phone calls and sleepless nights. Together that comes to a lot of trauma. The total number of disturbances (gets out pencil and paper) – 109 + 4 + 3 + 4 + 1 + 4 + 22 + 8 + 1 – not that they will ever match a dead fish on a window sill – comes to, mm, 156.

Linda on the other hand will involve: 0 emails, 0 architects' plans, 0 comments to council, 0 council decisions, 0 articles, 0 people contacted, 0 property visits, 0 phone calls, 0 sleepless nights. Total disturbances: 0.

I nudged Danny onto a piece of A4 paper and placed this on a window sill. I wondered if he had been reincarnated already. Possibly even as Linda, that may be her at the door.

Send me Linda, anyone but Mick and Melba – sounding like people in some fiction – Mick and Melba Brown, with their stupid names and stupid cars and stupid beard and silly arm-waving and shit style of walking, sort of zigzag, stupid stupid everywhere, from their stupid matching bobble hats to that weathervane they mentioned and grinned about the last time they came to the door, that ludicrous weathervane I've yet to see. Do I want to see it? I can't hear myself think. The song thrush has gone. The robins, starlings, magpies, even the pigeons. The fuck-all project harries and vexes anything that comes near, like a swan chasing a goose, in and out of water, not a comparison I'm comfortable with in front of Danny. I quietly tuck the thought of a swan chasing a goose away, under my breath, and have it fly off, taking its honking with it.

Poor Dan is dead, some paper holds his head, he looks so peaceful and serene.

This makes 157.

It is time for a service of remembrance for poor Danny, who was taken from us so young, so soon.

As you lie there on the wet stone, you and the stone both slowly drying, giving up a moisture which, let us imagine, will surely join its parts to become a single drop of rain, to fall hopefully in some place of dignity, a fine green sward of land, or past a white cliff into some noble body of water, I could see, Danny, you were truly fucked. Ignorance prevents me coming up with hard details, but how you'd been through the mill, only to perish in this brutal land of human disappointments. First your forebears had run so many gauntlets in the gulf-blown waters of north-east Mexico, only to be scooped up almost by accident – some were scooped and some were spared – and carried from their homes for ever, via cold-hearted dealers who in hardly a beat of their icy hearts kept decanting them in various containers before arranging that fateful flight over the Atlantic. Yes your forebears had their trauma too, removed far from their natural noble realm, cast up to jet above the clouds, hurtling east in darkness under stars they had no idea of, shaken and stilled by the shocks from takeoffs and landings, forklift trucks and container lorries, never to know they were also just part of one other great trauma, the centuries of tragedy and oppression, those open veins of Latin America. That's your background, Danny. Everyone has their background. But you were really out of luck. Once over their jet lag (do fish get jet lag?), your forebears may have languished in loft spaces in the Old Kent Road, before actually bearing young, who bore more young, which is where you came in, where I came in, as I'm hardly guiltless either, having brought you here when I should have set off with you, fish bowl under my arm, back across the Atlantic. What a contrast to the bombastic Browns that would have been, to have hired a quiet and ethnically correct boat to take you out and watch you splash back into the warm waters of the Laguna Madre, as far as possible from sharks and pelicans, Danny. To swim amongst the plants and fish, be part of the whole unravelling.

Psych

Eamon O'Riordan

Gary smiles from his ergonomic chair.

I remove my winter jacket to the hook behind the door, reaching in to kill my phone just as it starts buzzing from another call.

I sit down on the slightly less comfortable chair facing him.

These are my weekly appointments with Gary. Nicola's told me I must keep going no matter what.

After dawdling bromides on the eye-watering weather, I give him the spark notes on the week. The number of good days, the number of bad.

'How does it feel in those moments?' he asks, when I mention the bad.

I run my eyes over the distraction of pulp crime, Steinbeck, and Carl Jung that throng the shelves behind him, playing for time.

'Imagine the top of a lasagna left in the oven a little too long, the sizzle and burn of blisters forming, then you turn up the heat – you keep turning up the heat.'

'I see,' he says, a little less impressed with my analogy than I'd have liked.

'And when you feel this way, what do you do next?'

'Anything I can think of to make it stop.'

'Such as?'

I tell him about going deep into documentaries on the major turning points of the Second World War or the internecine intrigues of the early Saxon kings. My gifted copy of *Meditations* that I've barely skimmed. The hyper-edited YouTube clips of well-built males flexing on how even they've had struggles with their mental health.

He smiles, and waits, and listens, the spines of the crime novels glistening behind him.

'You mentioned last time you felt ready to start looking for a new job,' he says, 'or – that you might consider the old one again, can't remember which.'

I examine the ceiling fan above our heads, destined to remain dormant for months until the warm weather returns. I doubt I'll be ready even by then for the full-throttle office days that bleed into evenings and weekends.

'I've updated my resume, so yeah, soon.'

'That must feel like progress. And the pressure from the wedding planning is still there?'

The Tuscan wedding that drove me to the Director job in the first place. A honeymoon touring the lesser-known fishing villages south of Cinque Terre. Nicola's pick was Tellaro, mine Lerici. Everything onwards and upwards, until one of my direct reports found me sitting on the floor of my office, staring at the whiteboard in the twitching light. They had to call Nicola to take me home.

'Tuscany's still the plan,' I say.

He smiles again and waits.

Next, I take him on a diversion through one of my childhood memories, the airing of which we can pretend is meaningful and apt. Today it's me hiding in the cobwebbed garage from my father due home from the bar. Stood in my socks on the rippled cement, comparing the warning signs on the rusted tins of paint until I hear the door handle turn. In a rush he would be hugging me and telling me that I'm his very best boy, while I close my eyes and count to ten against his hokey claustrophobia of damp cigarettes and bargain-bin cologne.

'Very good,' he says, stressing the first syllable.

'Don't know why I even mentioned it.'

'It will be good to let yourself circle back to think about that over the next few days,' he says, before settling again into his waiting pattern.

I commit to doing this and divert again, this time providing him with examples pitched to assure him that I've a much better handle on stuff now.

I want him to know that he's helping, that he's doing a good job. He seems moderately pleased.

'I – I text random people I know,' I say then, suddenly raising the stakes.

'Oh,' he says, 'like who?'

'Whoever's showing online on WhatsApp or Instagram. Facebook, Telegram, other apps.'

'I see,' he says, pausing to look at his watch.

'Women most of the time.' Throb of exhilaration at finally saying it out loud.

'Women?'

He waits, looks at his watch again, and smiles.

'I don't know why it helps, but it does – the conversations, while they flow, take me out of my hundred-mile-an-hour, scattered ant thoughts.'

'This is great work,' he says.

I wait for him to prod and cajole, but all he does is smile and nod.

'I see we are at time,' he says eventually. 'Let's pick it up here next week.'

Next week, I'll be telling him, actually, the texting isn't all that bad. Next week, I might not even turn up.

'You're making good progress,' he says.

'Thanks, Gary,' I sigh, rising to free my coat from its hook. 'Nicola will be glad to hear it.'

Out on the street, I delete the texts from the women I've been chatting to. There are voicemails and missed call notifications from unsaved numbers; I delete those too. I zip the phone back into my jacket pocket, cross the busy street and take the quieter route home through the residential side streets lined with tall Victorian houses.

When I reach the entrance to our building, there's a limber fellow in a cerulean shell suit sitting on the wall swinging his feet. I tap my keycard to enter, and take the elevator to our floor without seeing anyone else.

After hanging my coat in the sector of wardrobe assigned to winter coats, I remove the wooden board from behind the placemats by the side of the fridge and the utility knife from the drawer and set about chopping garlic, shallots, and cilantro stems for a curry paste.

That night Nicola brought me home from the office we sat up late in bed talking for a long time. I told her about the corkscrew tightness in my chest and the days spent riding the subway to the end of the line instead of going to the office. She made me promise (i) to tell her everything always and (ii) let her find a professional for me to talk to. Her therapist aunt sent us a list of recommendations that I whittled down to Gary on the basis that his profile photo showed an unthreatening middle-aged man smiling and in front of a stocked bookshelf.

Chopping done, I throw the offcuts into the bulging garbage under the sink. Since they're both full, I take the organics and the regular garbage out to the hallway for the 30-second walk to the garbage chute. The chute is housed in the tiniest room in the building, with just enough space for all the necessary garbage movements.

I press the green button, pull the lever to lower its steel chin, then drop the food bag in. It slaps against the inside of the chute as it goes down before softly splodging onto the vast swollen belly of fragrant organics below. I press the red 'garbage' button, causing distant sounds of rearrangement to occur. When the light flashes, I drop that bag in. Its descent is markedly shrill by comparison and ends with the sound of something finally breaking.

I turn to open the door but it won't give, as if someone is holding it shut from the other side. I knock and say sorry a few times but there's no answer. I finally pull hard and the door is immediately released so that I'm thrown back against the chute-room wall. The man in the blue shell suit steps in from the hallway, chin protruding. He looks me up and down, then nods his head like he's agreeing with himself about something.

'I know you,' he says, jabbing his middle finger into my chest.

'Sorry, what?' I say.

'What?' he says 'What? Let's go with sending my kid sister photos of your limp dick,' he says, not looking like a person who wants to be reasoned with.

'I – I don't know what you're talking about,' I say, which for now, despite his evident certainty, is the truth.

'She's on meds,' he spits, 'and you won't leave her alone with your pathetic emo bullshit.'

His face is too close to mine now, all I see is nose and eye. I close my own eyes and turn my face away so that my cheek is flush to the smooth tiled wall.

'Nicola left you, eh?' he says, letting me know he's done his homework.

He dents his forehead against the side of my head, I can't think of anything useful to say. His breath's on my neck.

'Claire's not well,' he says, 'she asked you to stop.'

'I know, OK, I know,' remembering Claire now, brittle after being recently dropped by Justin, a graphic designer I barely knew from years ago. She'd complain about him for hours while sending me carefully filtered lewds for me to compliment. Sometimes we'd get each other off.

'So you remember now,' he says, grabbing a handful of my t-shirt. Then he lets me go and takes a step back towards the hallway, wedging a toe in the door to keep it from closing.

'I'm sorry, I'm going through a weird – please –'

The family from number 14 can be heard talking and laughing. I wonder now how much they've heard. He hears them too and his shoulders relax. It looks like their proximity might help take things down a notch.

'I promise,' I say, 'never again.'

'Well,' he says, 'she's changed her number now but if you slide into her socials, I'm going to DM Nicola, all your contacts, every single thing you sent.'

He shoves me once more then disappears round the corner to the elevators. I hear the relieving ding of doors opening, then wait another few minutes for my breath to calm to its regular rhythm.

I need some air. I take the stairs to the outdoor common area at the top of the building.

Out on the balcony, I lean bare-elbowed on the exterior railing and gulp the frigid air. The vents from the building's heating system whirr behind me. To the south, the strident office blocks of the financial district bristle square patches of light for the lawyers under the gun and the cleaners starting their shift.

One evening, months ago, when I was supposed to be at Gary's, Nicola came home early to find me still in bed with the covers pulled up to my chin. She told me that if I wasn't going to make an effort with the appointments, why should she kill herself every day at work worrying about me. I told her she had a point. And later, after things calmed down enough for us to agree on Thai takeout for dinner, I took a long shower to give her some space. But soon, the ugly sound of her crying from the bedroom told me that she'd found the texts and photos on my phone that I'd left under the pillow. She quietly told me through the shower curtain that we were done for good. Left for her mom's that night.

I can still convince myself that I'm feeling better. That soon I'll be ready to email the office to set up a date to return. And, after a month of demonstrating to everyone that I'm working normally like I used to do, I'll see if Nicola would meet for a coffee. I even remain convinced long enough to make me believe that this time it's going to stick. And it does stick, until from nowhere, again, things start to itch, and I'm pacing my 500-square-foot prison, scratching out texts to anyone I can think of that might be weaker than me.

Claire's brother should teach me a lesson. But I know tomorrow will be the same.

I hug my arms tight to my chest.

The vents continue to whirr. The night-time city blinks. Down below, the street is slick and the traffic is sparse.

The sign over the corner store buzzes epileptic. A bearded jogger runs under it, momentarily caught in the strobe.

Mind the Gap

Ellen Kelly

She lets Billy have her bedroom for his first session.

'This costs two euros a minute. Make the most of every second,' she says as a joke to relax him but wants to take it right back when she sees the smile, a resigned half smile which seems to say, *Yes, Mum, I know I'm a burden.*

Below in the living room she hears her lock slide across and then click into place, in a swift decisive movement. A good sign. Then the creak of her chair as he rolls it along the floorboards to her desk, adjusts it down with a clunk to suit his height, followed by a pause as she imagines him positioning himself in front of his screen, fixing his headphones on. She checks the time. 15.59. That last excruciating minute before a make or break exam she tries not to think, but there it is anyway, thrumming in her, as she paces up and down on the red rug beside the hearth.

She hears it kick off with that first word, the introduction, an assent of sorts. At last, she thinks. Here it is. She settles herself on the couch directly below him. His voice trembles through the floor and down onto her head, indistinct words swirling, vibrating, melodious. She sinks further, propping her face on the turquoise velvet cushion, feeling a little drugged as she listens to the lilt of his voice and then to the gaps, like a train coming in to the station, settling for a moment and then off again. The rhythm is hypnotic. She can make out a word or two after the gaps.

Exactly.

No, no.

Yes.

Staccato notes. Exactly what, she wonders. And exactly how has this therapist, meeting her son for the first time, online, managed to grasp it?

She looks up at the spot on the ceiling where Billy had once flung a glow-in-the-dark yellow sticky stress ball. It had stayed up there for days, defying gravity, staring viciously at her, judging her as the evenings rolled in and the light dimmed. In the end she had roared at him to get the horrible thing down. A little bit of alarm danced in his soft hazel eyes, as it sometimes did in their interactions. And if it leaves a bloody mark up there, she had continued, knowing she should stop, now, she really should, there'll be murder, you know that, don't you?

The grey stain that remained these past six years is a slyer kind of judge, she thinks now, like an eye, squinting, pretending to be closed, or else winking at her, a mocking wink, seeing it all.

It had to be a female therapist, Billy told her, and she had taken this as a compliment of sorts, that he thinks women are more empathetic, better listeners, more understanding. She could be all of those things, too, at times. She has her moments when empathy triumphs over low pulsing anxiety and they are at one, in the flow of life, a great little team. Like that time with the mouse. The house had been infested. They were getting in behind the fridge, up through the walls at night and out into the bedrooms, escalating her insomnia, driving her right to the edge. Peanut butter traps were set, corpses bagged and binned by her husband in pragmatic sweeps against the tide. One evening, passing the bin outside, Billy thought he heard a little squealing noise. He lifted the lid and opened the plastic bag to discover a not-so-dead mouse, pinned by its leg in the trap, black searching eyes. He went to his father about it who told him not to worry, it would be dead soon or else he could hurry it along, take a spade to it if that's what Billy wanted. It is not what Billy wanted. What he did want was to know how the hell his father could bin a little creature when it was still alive? And what was he supposed to do, now, with this fresh information?

'We have to save it,' Billy said in a whisper to his mother and she had looked at him in a quizzical way at first, but somehow knew to be careful this time and not to say the obvious thing, that they had been killing them for months, that saving them wasn't on the agenda, as such.

'How?' she had asked instead, trying not to add that they can't exactly take it along to the vet or call animal rescue.

'We'll drive away from here, down to the woods and set it free,' he said simply, and seemed to brace himself with a deep breath and rapid blinking, waiting for the retort that would most naturally come to her, trip off her tongue, sharp and stingy. She pushed it down.

'Okay then,' she said and he smiled, the star-shaped dimple beneath his left eye deepening.

They snuck out in the dark of night, Billy with the supermarket bag containing the half-killed mouse on his knee, and she drove off, feeling the madness of it but something else too as the cries of the mouse pierced them both. At the edge of the woods she watched him do it, open the trap, talking to the mouse like an old friend as he did so. The mouse lay there at first, unwilling to be saved only to be eaten by something else – she'd lie there too if she were him – but he sprang up then out of the trap and looked all around, looked at her son with shiny, furtive, grateful eyes and hobbled off into the woods. She felt a tear loosen and run a hot path down her right cheek. She wanted that mouse to survive as much as he did.

The gaps are getting longer. That therapist must be doing a lot of the talking. Isn't it supposed to be the other way around? Unless he's upset and the therapist is sitting with it, holding him there, well able for it, she thinks, as a shudder runs through her, remembering her own response when he told her. Quick-fire solutions, tamping it down, batting it away. His voice again now, vibrating on through to her body below. She listens for the words that must be there, somewhere in the soup, or else readying to come out. What will they sound like now? Muffled or clear, ambiguous or precise?

*

Picking up her phone, she sees it's 16.21. A third of the way in to the session. She sends a text to her husband – *Call me* – and her phone dutifully chimes a minute later. She puts it on speaker, turns the volume right up and leaves it to ring for as long as she can so that Billy might hear it above too. Then she answers just before it cuts off.

'You okay?' he asks, high-pitched, like a car alarm.

'Yes,' she shouts back for Billy's ears, and she laughs. 'Everything is good.'

'I got a fright there for a minute with your message, then the delay?'

'Exactly. No, no. Yes.'

'What?'

'Absolutely. For sure.'

She was hoping for a bit more of a cheerful flow up through the ceiling to Billy, sing-song banter, encouraging him along. It was her mistake to rile her husband with the urgency of *Call me*. And now it will be near on impossible to claw back, he'll question and prod and she'll pull herself further in.

'Is Billy there? Put him on to me, will you?'

She presses *end call* and places the phone on airplane mode while merry chit-chat streams out of her as if it's late in the day and she's sitting at a bar with her great friend from her school days. How she'd love that. The last time they spoke was very different though. A phone call looking for advice, spilling the words quickly, hearing the click of a lighter, the pull and the puff of smoke. She pictured her friend's bright, kind eyes as the words hit and she heard her then in the gap that followed, taking an extra-long drag of the cigarette, puffing it out and saying *oh god*. She fired the questions anyway. Should they report it to the police? What happens after? Should they take a case? How does that work? She jotted down the answers in bullet points as if drawing up a shopping list. Then she listened to the summary.

'You can do all those things, sure. If you were a client I'd be advising you to. Knowing you, though, as I do, I wonder. You're soft, gentle. He's like you, isn't he? Would you be able for a protracted process, full of uncertainty? Would he?'

She was surprised at how her friend described her, she didn't know that this is how people saw her. Nor that Billy is thought to be like her. She'd like to be a bit more like him, truth be told.

'I've seen what it can do,' her friend had continued.

'The years in limbo as it invades every little thing. Then once it begins, all the doubt-casting by the defence. It can destroy even the most robust people.'

She jotted *robust* down.

'And they'd most likely go after why he continued there, during the period of harassment and especially after the assault.'

The words didn't sound so bad by themselves, without the word that should be in front of them both. Her friend couldn't bring herself to say it either.

'Why didn't he leave what was just a summer job, if it was so traumatic?'

There it was. The clincher. She pictured Billy's shaking hands as he attempted to do his electric blue tie for his next shift and how she had taken over, flipping and folding with efficiency as she talked to him. He shouldn't run. He should stay. He should report it to the owner. There would be procedures. It could stop this happening to other young people.

He did as she said.

But she was wrong.

It was a trap.

And she had set it.

*

There's a single orange in the fruit bowl hidden underneath a bunch of leopard-dotted bananas. Plucking it out, she digs her thumb into the coarse skin, releasing a light misty citric spray up into the air. She peels off a nice little curved bumpy road of skin and drops it into a crystal tumbler before going to the cabinet and pulling out the gin, vermouth and Campari. The joy of having it all in the one place. Except the ice. She'll have to leave the living room and go to the kitchen for that, risk not hearing him. There's a gap. She makes a dash for the fridge, chatting all the way and then back with the ice tray in hand. Silence still. She bangs the tray hard onto the table and ice cubes spring out, bouncing in all directions, some landing on the floor. The creak of her chair rolling above. He heard the bang. He's worried. But he needs to focus so she chit-chats on, raising her voice. Scooping some loose cubes from the table, she chucks them into her glass with the orange peel and splashes the three liquids in on top, equal parts, or thereabouts. She picks up a navy pen from the table, one of the college societies he had joined in freshers' week, before he dipped out. She plunges it into the liquid and stirs, watching the red ascend and infuse, spreading like an exotic sunrise.

His last word vibrates down to her, dancing on her crown. A long minute passes before the lock on her door slides back across. She sucks the sweet, bitter dregs from around the melting ice and waits for the sound of his footfall on the stairs.

Dutch Angle

Jennifer McMahon

Charged air as if before a storm, this feeling creeping over him of a thing to come which cannot yet be seen, only silver light in a tight beam to say that this is a moment when something is bound to happen, if not this one then the next, but it is coming. He is alone in the jittery privacy of anticipation, seats arrayed on either side and to front and back, breathless in the wait, the wine gum between his thumb and forefinger poised before his mouth and growing sticky, the way some things stick to you and never let go, the loss of a child and the leaving of a woman, the impatient falling and dying away of his world, nothing existing now but the silver beam and a swarm of dust motes pivoting through it like memories he'd rather forget, but there is no forgetting those things that shaped him and brought him to this place, his father calling to him from the projection booth, his dead father who's been stretched in his grave these last six months, calling to him to say, 'Are you ready, Danny?'

And now it comes, this thing he's been waiting for, this replaying of the entire expanse of his life, the joy and the pain, the birth and the dying, the living, breathing, plotless mess of a man who's seen better days and has known far worse, numbers counting down on the screen as the reel turns towards what cannot be avoided. He closes his eyes, comes to fire within himself, this frothing anger that has dogged him for forty years, because it is mean, this life we're given, so mean and so awfully unfair.

Weather falls thick on Kilcronin in barrelling leaves of gold and mottled green, their best given, now the life is dying out of them as late autumn blusters through branches so recently heaved with summer growth. Every year, it happens, and every year, the community is surprised. It's cold for the time of year, they say, and the nights are drawing in. They say it as if the light will never come again, as if this is the final darkening of the world and the ending of all things loved and known.

Danny O'Driscoll walks the night, heedless of the storm. It's a wild one, the tail-end of an Atlantic bruiser shearing hard across the west of Ireland, but the date is what it is and can't be changed. If a storm should fall on this night, he must endure it. This is his annual pilgrimage to converse with the dead, but it is not to the graveyard he goes. His destination is the shell of the Silver Palace, the Silly as it was known in his youth, long shut down and left to ruin.

The whole town laughed and cried there at one time or another, stole first kisses, threw kung fu shapes after watching Bruce Lee, or drew fast after a Clint Eastwood. They travelled shoulder to shoulder along a ribbon of silver dreams, cheering on heroes and booing villains, sitting on the edges of their seats and yearning for the climax but not yet, not yet. To look at it now, boarded up and charred by a fire ten years ago, the walls scrawled with lurid graffiti – to look at these things, they should feel nothing but shame.

There's talk of the Silly being torn down, and a block of apartments being built in its place, like the ones they built last year at the top of the town. Such is progress, and the powerful, those who develop and take brown envelopes full with promises, they clap each other on the back for their initiative and daring, deeming their vision to be bold, while they drive around in their fancy cars and devour their young. His anger rising, he makes a fist and shakes it at the sky, all the better to relish his indignation. If the Silly should go, what will he do? What has he ever done but trudge from day to day, a shadow of what was long ago a happy man.

Gaining access is no easy thing. The gate at the side of the cinema is padlocked, but it helps him get purchase on the supporting wall. Child's play for an agile teenager, but to a weary man, it's a grunting, groaning challenge. Then there's the prising of the boards on the side door, enough to allow him entry. He takes a torch from his coat pocket as he enters a dark corridor. The air has a pet-shop smell, rats or mice. A litter of crushed beer cans crowds the end of the corridor. He brushes them aside, and opens the door into the theatre, then lifts his gaze to the square hole high up in the wall at the back, the location of the projection booth from which he and his father watched all the classics together.

It was the atmosphere of *The Third Man* that struck him the most, the scene on the Ferris wheel, Harry Lime looking down on the people below as he mused about their unimportance. What would it matter, he asked, if this one or that one died? Dutch angle; the term comes back to Danny now, the way they filmed some scenes at a slant to portray how Lime was at odds with the world he lived in.

Halfway up the centre aisle, he finds a seat that wasn't too badly damaged in the fire. He's about to sit when something rustles in the next row, too big to be a rat. A ruffled head pops up, and two eyes squint in the torchlight. 'Who's there?' Danny says, then, 'Duster?'

'Danny?'

'Aye, it's me. What're you doing here?'

Duster sits up and stretches. 'Getting in out of the storm.'

'I thought you were in the homeless shelter.'

'I was, but they caught me bringing a bottle in.' He pauses, then leans closer and lowers his voice. 'Why're you here?'

'The date,' Danny says, taking his seat.

'Ah, okay. Already?'

'Time flies.'

'Depends,' Duster says. He nods to the screen. 'We had some fun here, right? Back in the day. The movies we saw. Your old man was great, I was sorry to hear he passed. Your mother, too. You're the unluckiest son of a ...' He covers his eyes, gives himself a shake. 'I'm sorry. Don't mind what I say. I'm drunk.'

'Aren't you always?'

'Not half enough, by my measure. Do you want privacy?'

'No, you can stay. We were friends once.'

Duster's expression is pained. 'Are we not still?'

Danny shrugs. 'I suppose we are. I've not had many since ... you know.'

'It was a sad day.'

'And the sadness grows. Give me a moment.'

Danny sits and stares to the front, where the tattered and burnt remains of red curtains still hang in places. The silver screen is gone, but the dream comes back to him, the beam of light and the lifetime of memories it carried. His father's voice too, always soft and never scolding, not like his mother, the harder of the pair. If there was meaning to what his father showed him, he can't see it, only the rehashing of what he can't forget. An accident, not

Danny's fault but perhaps he wasn't paying enough attention. His son was in the back, strapped in and safe until the moment he wasn't, and then he was gone for good. A drunk driver hit them on Sean's side of the car, right where he was sitting. The guard said it was instant, and he'd not have suffered. Stella couldn't take the grief, and couldn't bear to look at Danny a moment longer.

'I'm sorry,' he says, then there are tears in his eyes, drenching his face, the sobs tearing at his throat as his words come hoarse and hot. 'Sweet Jesus, I'm sorry.'

It has to be here, where his father worked and his mother came often, their home away from home where he brought Sean to watch movies old and new, regardless of his age, and if he didn't understand them then, he would someday. Continuity is important, even if it's meaningless these days.

'Can I do anything to help?' Duster says after a while, his voice low.

Danny shakes his head, draws a sleeve across his nose. 'No one can.' He regards Duster, the mottled coat too thin to keep winter at bay, his unshaven jaw, the beaten look of a man who's falling fast and probably doesn't care. 'How's your mother?'

'Still alive, but I've not spoken to her in ages.'

'How'd you come to this, Duster?'

'Little by little. I'd no great plan for it.'

'You're not getting any younger.'

'Neither are you, Danny. I hear they're going to turn this place into apartments. O'Riordan's firm, the usual boyos. He'll make a packet, and the same man wouldn't toss me a bit of change if he saw me on the street. What will you do when it's gone?'

'Struggle on, I suppose, same as I always have.'

'We've lost the world we knew.'

'Men like us have always been at a slant to it. I had a dream about the Silly, last night.'

'A good one?' Duster says.

'No, or maybe. I don't know. Did you eat today?'

'Yesterday, I think. It's hard to remember.'

'Other things can't be forgotten.'

'True enough,' Duster says, 'but maybe we're not meant to forget them. Like old films, and each time you see them, you find something new. I remember all the ones your father showed us. They still play in my mind, some nights.'

Silence falls between them, the silence before a show when the audience is settled in and breathless, waiting for the first scene and the introduction of characters they've yet to know, but by the end of the night, they'll be like friends to them. The best ones will stick with them their whole lives.

'Duster?'

'Hmm?'

'Come on away with me. The house above is empty, I'm rattling around in it on my own. We'll have a decent supper, and talk of how things were.'

Duster straightens up, a large man when he's not bent and beaten from living and alcohol. 'Are you sure?'

'Gather what little you have. There's a warm bed waiting for you.'

A bottle, a bag of nothings, Duster stands and clutches them to his chest. 'You're a good friend, Danny, always were.'

'Tell me, Duster, did you ever hear of a thing called Dutch angle?'

'Can't say I have. What is it?'

'It's us. You and me in a changing world.'

Many years pass and draw down, and there's talk in Kilcronin of the apartments on the site of the old cinema being haunted. The occupants complain of voices in the night, a searing silver beam, a tappa-tappa which always seems to come from behind. All they know is that it's there, as are the ghosts of a boy and his father, appearing as if seated together, their eyes glowing. Sitting with them is a dishevelled man who likes to laugh. The ghosts aren't unfriendly, the residents are quick to add, but they paid enough for their apartments and the least they expected was a decent night's sleep without this sort of nonsense.

The older townsfolk smile knowingly, and some will, from time to time, shed a tear. 'It's only Danny and his boy, God rest them,' they say. 'And Duster along with them, didn't Danny take him home and care for him to the end of his days and ease his own grief by doing so? Let them have their fun. They suffered enough in this world, and they deserve a bit of joy in the hereafter.'

'It's not fair,' the complainants say.

The reply comes, tolerant and amused. 'And what in God's good world ever is?'

The Beard

Moya Roddy

A body tumbled, spiralling helplessly down a deep black hole. Paul Sinclair jerked awake. It wasn't the sensation of falling that had awoken him but the look on the face of the person falling, someone he recognised as himself. There was something so bald in the expression, so exposed, it appalled him. In an effort to shake off the feeling, he yawned, raising his hands to rub sleep from his eyes. As he did so, he became aware in a slow, sickening way of something soft and hairy touching his palms. He screamed.

Paul stared into the mirror. What he was seeing was impossible. Yet there it was: the lower half of his face covered in a soft, black beard. He gave it a tug, expecting it to come away in his hand. When it didn't he told himself it had to be a trick. But how? Who? He lived alone, had spent the previous evening working in his study then gone to bed. He tugged again but no matter how hard he pulled, the thing refused to budge; the skin underneath reddening, making him wince. Paul took a deep breath. There had to be an explanation, beards don't suddenly appear. He shoved his face closer. He'd always been clean shaven, in fact disliked beards, although he had to admit this was a particularly fine one. Well cared for. Groomed. He pressed his nose to the glass. Could he be experiencing some sort of amnesia? Was the reflection in the mirror his? Of course it was, he'd know his eyes anywhere. And his hair. A photograph! Why hadn't he thought of it sooner! Impatiently, Paul went from room to room pulling open drawers, although he realised almost immediately it was going to prove a waste of time. There weren't any recent photos. He'd got rid of the few there were, tore them up in a fit of rage when things soured between him and Jean. Deleted the ones she'd sent to his BlackBerry. At the thought of his phone another fear began to plague him. What if his voice sounded different? To be on the safe side, he turned off his mobile and for a moment felt almost naked.

'Nonsense!' he exclaimed out loud, returning to the idea of amnesia. He knew who he was! He was Paul Sinclair, CEO of Emerald Holdings, their offices – quickly Paul scribbled his personal details on the back of an envelope before hurrying to his study. Picking up a business card – the firm's logo clear as daylight – his name, position and mobile number exactly as he'd jotted them down. He slumped in a chair, bewildered. Perhaps he'd been working too hard – it had been a source of friction between him and Jean, he had to admit; she complaining he'd no time for her, or rather, didn't make time. A loud ringing invaded his ears. I'm losing it, he thought, then realised it was the landline on his desk that was making the racket. He hadn't heard it for so long; he'd forgotten what it sounded like. Who on earth could be calling him? Nobody used landlines anymore; he only kept his out of sentimentality. The ringing stopped then started up again almost immediately. Hesitating, he picked it up; he could always plead a sore throat.

'Paul? Is that you? Your mobile was off. I was worried.'

It was Alex, his secretary, no doubting her voice. Paul grunted in response, afraid to trust what might come out.

'Miley emailed. He's coming today, 3.15.'

The person she was referring to was George Miley of GM Construction, the company on the other end of the proposed acquisition. That's what he'd been working on last night, all year in fact. He was going to shaft Miley and he wasn't looking forward to it.

Realising Alex was expecting a response, he mumbled something incoherently.

'Are you alright? You sound – '

Sweat broke out on Paul's forehead. He took a deep breath. 'I-I-, I'm fine. A bit of a throat ... Did he say if he was coming alone?'

'He is. His nephew's been held up in Dubai.'

'That's wonderful – I mean, thank you, Alex. Thank you.'

'See you shortly.'

As the line went dead his secretary's words reverberated round his head: 'See you shortly!' Instinctively, his fingers went to his chin. Feeling the thick, silky hair, he let out a groan.

Paul paced the room. In an old medical dictionary he'd found an entry for what was termed 'partial amnesia' but it seemed ludicrous a person could forget something as obvious as a beard while remembering every other facet of their life. Suddenly he laughed. What an idiot! What a complete and utter idiot! Nothing could be simpler. It was so bloody obvious he'd almost missed it. On his way to the bathroom Paul gave a little whoop, then his own version of a high five; he'd have jumped if his bulk permitted. He must make a note to get back on his diet, lose a bit of weight. That was something else Jean was always going on about. If one of his staff had taken this long to come up with a solution he'd have fired him. At the words, Paul's new-found relief evaporated. Damn it, he'd almost forgotten his 12 o'clock appointment! The meeting with Coyne and what's-his-name Heaney wasn't going to be pleasant. What was the term they used in America? Downsizing. It didn't have the same nasty ring as redundancy. The Americans were good at that kind of thing. Still, it had to be done, with this latest acquisition in the pipeline the company needed to shed deadweight. It was bad luck it had to be those two, worse luck he was the one who was going to have to break the news. Well, at least this other little problem had been solved: shave the damned thing off, simple as that! And if anyone commented he'd claim he'd gotten fed up with the damn thing, and if no one did – he'd better make an appointment to see a specialist.

Paul regarded the shaving implements lined up in front of him. What the hell was stopping him? Here was the solution and for some reason he was hesitating. Why, for God's sake? For some strange reason, now he had the beard he found the idea of parting with it difficult. He didn't feel he'd the right to just, well, get rid of it. Stop being a fool, he told himself, reaching for a pair of scissors.

It was no use. Before he took such drastic action he needed to know how long he'd had the beard and why. Besides – here his heart beat a little faster – what if he'd always had it and really had forgotten? Sitting on the edge of the bath, he stroked the beard. It felt so right, so reassuring, as if it had been lying in store a long time, waiting.

Hearing the door to his apartment open, Paul froze. Moments later, a humming sound filled the air and he recognised the tuneless voice of his cleaning lady, Sally. Panic-stricken, he reached for the razor, then remembered he hadn't seen her for several months. He could have grown a beard in that time. Gingerly, Paul stepped into the hallway.

'Oh,' Sally screamed, seeing him. 'Mr Sinclair! You gave me such a fright!'

Paul opened his mouth to explain.

'I thought the place was empty,' she continued, struggling to put her coat back on, without giving his beard as much as a second glance. 'I can come back later.'

'Oh – that won't be necessary. I'm-I'm on my way to the office. Sally?'

She glanced at him expectantly.

He opened his mouth, shut it. 'Nothing. By the way,' he added, 'I'd prefer if you didn't disturb things in my study.'

There was a moment's silence. 'You're the boss,' she sniffed.

Picking up his briefcase, Paul let himself out. He'd been meaning to say that to her for quite some time.

As soon as the door closed behind his two now ex-employees, Paul poured himself a whiskey, drank it in one go and poured another. He swivelled in his chair, savouring the taste. As he'd expected, they'd tried the 'last in, first out' card but he'd held his nerve, explained the old adage no longer applied. These days, younger men had the advantage; experience no longer a major factor. What was essential was adaptability, flexibility, things that decreased as one got older. A fact of life. Business life anyway. He'd anticipated their arguments, out-manoeuvred them. More to the point, he'd enjoyed it. Yes, he had to admit, he'd derived a certain feeling of satisfaction from the whole proceedings. He must be toughening up. After all, he'd known these men since he began working for the company; had met their wives at company functions. His hand went to his face. Stupid as it seemed, he felt the beard had helped. The whole thing was bizarre. He couldn't claim to understand it. No one, not one single person, had commented on it. It was as if he'd always had it. But he'd stake his life it hadn't been there yesterday. Was he going mad? He didn't feel mad. He felt alive, powerful. He'd even begun looking forward to George Miley's visit. Paul drained his glass. Something was happening all right. And whatever it was, he liked it.

Paul leaned back in his chair. What Miley was saying was true, the price Emerald was offering for GM was derisory, well below the company's worth. He also knew it didn't matter. The other man would accept. This was a bit of game-playing. GM Construction had over-reached itself; was in hock up to its eyeballs. If it went bust it could bring the whole of Miley's empire with it. Of course, once Emerald acquired it, they'd sell off chunks, anything profitable – when the dust settled. Paul allowed himself a smile at the pun.

There would have to be massive redundancies of course, even at management level. Miley knew this but as Paul heard his own voice mouthing the platitudes and false promises essential to the other man's acceptance of the deal, as he outlined plans for 'sensitive reconstruction', 'worker consultation', he realised the embarrassment he'd expected to feel wasn't there. And although it was obvious from the glint in Miley's eyes that the older man saw right through him, Paul was conscious of something else – a sort of naked admiration in the other man's expression. Face it, he thought, Miley hadn't got where he was without dirtying his hands. There was recognition in that look of a fellow player.

'We'll get our lawyers busy on the paperwork, hammer out the finer details before the extraordinary general meeting. You've come a long way,' he added as they shook hands. Paul acknowledged the remark with a nod. When he'd started in the business, it was men like George Miley he'd secretly admired, watched, imitated.

'Why don't we have a drink and a bite to eat? There are a few ... things I'd like to discuss with you.'

Ensconced in the lounge of one of the better hotels, Paul was taken aback to see Jean coming through the revolving doors. She was looking straight at him but when he lifted a hand in greeting she walked straight past.

'Someone you know?' Miley asked.

Paul didn't answer. He was on his feet, intending to go after her, perhaps suggest they meet up later. Catching sight of his reflection in a large bevelled mirror on the far side of the room, he changed his mind.

'No, actually. I thought it was someone else,' he said, sitting down.

'By the way,' Miley commented. 'You should keep the beard, it suits you.'

Paul only half heard him. His eyes were following Jean but she was already disappearing through another set of doors.

Claw

Mauk Donnabhain

The old man's skin is brown and soft to the touch. Sagging around the waist, the grey hair on his chest pressed down with sweat. His face is like a piece of leather being polished. A shoeshine adventure in flesh and bones. There's something wrong about 'doing it' in the child's bedroom. The plush toys falling to the floor. Old-fashioned teddy bears. A twisted safari of tigers, giraffes, and elephants.

It reminds you of something; ponies and unicorns. Miniature cats, in suits and bow ties.

It's warm in the room, and painful, as he moves around on top of you. His hand rises up to grip the wall above your head, then it slowly moves down, mechanically clenching your throat. You can taste whiskey on his tongue, which is probing behind your teeth.

How did you even get here?

A day out in town. Book-buying, and a milkshake. Vanilla is the only flavour you'd really want. Hitching back home in the rain. It's winter, dark at half-past three, and the headlights whizz past like the eyes of predators reflected in patches of rain on the road ahead. When his car stops, you feel for the comfort of metal in your pocket.

His car is flashy. A personalised numberplate that you recognise, and the hard black and red cowhide interior. The smell of the man, as you climb into the front passenger seat. You know of him, but you don't yet know him. He's one of the richest men in the county. The casino owner; enemy, the destroyer of lives. You know his shame, and yet here he is, just an ordinary man in front of you. Older than you thought he would be, and he seems kind at first, like he really just wants to give you a lift.

'Are you local?'

He wouldn't know you. To him, you're just another wayward teenager; someone who should know better than to get into a car with a stranger. His daughter is just a few years older than you. She's at university, somewhere far away, but you've seen her in church. Impossibly pale, as though she's never spent time outdoors. As though she's never run through a field with the dogs or searched for lost coins on the riverbank. You wouldn't know the first thing to say to her, and that's the honest truth.

'You're awfully quiet!'

There's a moment to save the situation. To turn this back into a friendly lift home from a neighbour. You feel for the metal in your pocket and resolve to push this forward. You smile at him, like there's no danger at all in the situation.

'I'm a wee bit shy!'

The words have an effect on him, and he openly looks down at your crotch. The ripped jeans, and the hair on your skin bristling, when he puts his hand on your right leg.

'Well, we'll need to do something about that!'

***

Something to be reminded of. A late-night argument. A crashing sound in the room downstairs. Noises barely keep you awake these days. Fumbling in the early morning light, and laughter when you open your eyes, then close them again. Waking up in a bed full of colours. Pink and blue. Soft brown and neon green. Several dozen plastic eyes, watching you, waiting for a reaction. You've never seen so many soft toys in one place. It feels like Christmas has come unexpectedly, although it's still November. You arrange them in rows, give them names, draw up a rollcall. Five bears, two ponies, three cats, six types of dog, a camel, a snake, and a fish even! Where did they come from?

'The teddy-bear machine.'

Your mother looks sad, even though it's the best thing that's ever happened. Your father asks you to repeat the names. He has a glint in his eye, as he smiles from ear to ear.

You wonder whatever happened to all those toys. The excitement lasted a few days, barely even a week, before they were forgotten about. Staring silently from the top of the dresser, their eyes reproachful, as you grew up and moved onto more exciting things. They're no longer there. Your mother must have taken them down. Packed them away somewhere, passed them onto your younger cousins, or handed them in to the charity shop.

***

When it's all over, the old man looks ashamed. He puts his trousers back on and buttons up his shirt.

'I'll take you home.'

His idea of generosity, no doubt, but this isn't what you wanted. To leave his world so quickly, without time to find his weakness.

You accept the towel, when he hands it to you, and you mop up the mess he's created, as you sit upright on the bed. You see the soft toys on the floor, but you won't pick them up. You'll leave them there, as evidence of your presence in his life.

You wonder where his wife is. Where the younger child is. His daughter must be back at university, or on her big backpacking trip. She never accepted your Friend request, so you hear about her travels from other people. You could ruin it all for them. Go to the police. But would they even believe you?

Dressed now, you make your way downstairs, and he's standing in the hallway.

'Where is it you live again?'

He wouldn't know his way around your estate, despite the fact that it's people on your estate who have been pumping money into his bottomless machines. Your anger rises, and you feel for the metal in your pocket again. Still there. You think about all the lives he's ruined. Fathers gone. Families collapsed in on themselves. Now would be the perfect time. They would never believe that you were there in the first place. They would never understand how such a respectable businessman could end up bleeding to death in his own hallway. It would be a quick twenty minutes through the fields to your estate. No-one in the estate would question you. If they saw you coming through the hedge with a look of fear on your face, they'd never remember it afterwards.

He shifts nervously from one foot to the other. Perhaps he's seen it in your eyes, or he's just impatient to get you out of the house. He smiles broadly and puts a hand on your shoulder.

'You're really just delightful ... such a lovely young man!'

And the moment passes. You're not cut out for this. You loosen your grip on the metal in your pocket and dip your eyes, so he can't get inside your head again.

'The Fullwell Estate. You can drop me at the entrance to Moor Street.'

nOn-standard

Phil Cummins

'Cheeky little fecker! What's this *we* nonsense?' Re-reading the e-mail, he never ceased to wonder at the out-and-out brazenness of some students:

Dear Professor Gilmore,
The university has informed me that I am to be de-registered and must now withdraw from the degree programme because of my failing maths grades. As my course director, I need to meet with U as a matter of urgency to discuss how we are going to deal with this.
O.
Sent from my iPhone

Alan Gilmore heaped a palmful of aspirin into his mouth, sending a lukewarm slug of coffee in after them as he savoured the bitter smack on his tongue, jazz softly riffing from the battered radio next to his computer. Grey-haired, jowly, morose, the eyes hanging out of his head, he drew in a long deep breath and exhaled, massaging the bridge of his nose between forefinger and thumb.

'*We're* not dealing with anything, mate!' he grumbled, returning his gaze to the screen. 'You're the eejit who failed. And just how the bloody hell am I supposed to know who *O* is anyway?'

Try as he might, he couldn't put a face to the e-mail address. His head was all over the place, his thoughts jammed up like an M50 tailback. An image materialised in the throbbing space behind his eyes of some lazy, entitled tosser – an Orlando or an Oisín – sprawled languidly along the length of a soft sofa in t-shirt and sweats with a maths book open in his lap whilst texting away to his classmates about that miserable wanker of a lecturer, not a pen, calculator or notepad in sight, bare feet perched up on the radiator and head lolling back into the deep comfy folds of the cushion. With eyes occasionally glazing over as earbuds vibrated tinnily against his eardrums, the little git would be oblivious to the world, the equations on the page about as remote as an alternate universe.

'Mathematics is an exacting endeavour,' Gilmore had patiently lectured his students, 'one that demands absolute attention to detail.' But when it came to his beloved subject he felt that most of them these days had abandoned themselves to mediocrity.

'Whoever put the M in STEM never tried teaching maths to this shower,' chirped Bradshaw, drawing raucous hoots of laughter from around their lunch table only weeks earlier, Gilmore included.

'Fuck sake, Alan,' he muttered grimly as this last thought flashed through his sleep-deprived brain. 'When did you become so damn cynical?'

Sighing, he tapped out a brief reply confirming for two o'clock before leaning back and entrusting his headache to the therapeutic thrum of Charlie Haden's double bass.

'COME IN!' Gilmore boomed. Oliver Prendergast was late. He bustled into the office at two-fifteen, an overstuffed satchel hanging from his broad shoulder and a well-thumbed novel tucked under his damp armpit, and plunked himself down. An awkward, hefty, moon-faced yoke, plain as porridge, he had a clatter of bright red pimples scattered poppy-like across his pale chubby cheeks and a spiky brown fuzz on his upper lip that could've been usefully introduced to a disposable razor. Gilmore turned around from his computer fully prepared to berate his young visitor's tardiness when his gaze fell upon *The Hat*. It was an all too familiar jet black wide-brimmed fedora perched at a jaunty angle on Prendergast's round puddingy head. Gilmore groaned inwardly.

He immediately recalled the first time he'd spotted that hat in his lecture hall, its wearer always sitting in the front row utterly engrossed in that very same doorstopper of a Sci-Fi novel, humming away unselfconsciously to himself and occasionally scribbling little doodles into the margins of his book, seemingly unaware of the quarantine zone of empty seats around him or of the lesson unfolding before him. He'd initially tried to engage Prendergast by getting him up to the blackboard to complete a maths problem only for the lad to promptly seal up like a clam, his panicky face flushing wetly. Stubbornly snubbing the proffered chalk, his eyes had refused to meet Gilmore's, choosing instead to focus on some spot just over his right shoulder as if silently communing with his shadow. Gilmore decided it best to move on and recruit a more willing volunteer.

Detaining him some weeks later, Gilmore enquired, 'So, how're you finding the course? Attempted any of the sample problems yet?'

'Yes,' came Prendergast's soft reply, his lumpish frame awkwardly hugging his battered novel to his chest like a shield.

'Aaannnd ....?' Gilmore continued, eyebrows raised in hopeful anticipation. But Prendergast seemed averse to making eye contact or to elaborating beyond basic monosyllabic answers, Gilmore's ensuing questions simply rolling off him like water over a stone. He decided to change tack.

'So, tell me ... Oliver, isn't it? What's the book?'

Prendergast appeared to brighten up. '*House of Leaves*,' he replied. 'It's one of my favourite books. I've read it nine times. Have you ever read it?'

Gilmore replied that he had not. 'I don't suppose there's any maths in it?' he then asked. Clearly immune to sarcasm, Prendergast simply nodded and continued on his way.

What's going on inside that head of yours? Gilmore wondered as he watched the lad walk away.

Over the next two years Gilmore caught regular glimpses of that hat around the campus, its wearer always seeming to be on the periphery of things, attempting to osmose into the student body and take on the colour of belonging. But Prendergast was invariably regarded by students and staff alike as something of an oddity. An other.

Seated alone during lectures, the lad's remote demeanour made it difficult for Gilmore to gauge his abilities and teach him. Always he projected this aura of separateness. Gilmore had been informed early on that Prendergast was on a spectrum of some kind, although he privately detested such labels; they were unhelpful and smacked of convenience, he felt. That said, their conversations were invariably awkward and despite his best efforts the lad seemed disinclined to focus and put the work in, dooming him to consistently failing maths grades and an ensuing academic limbo that prevented him from moving forward. Gilmore eventually wrote him off as a lost cause, as something unfathomable.

And now Prendergast sat before him in the office, forehead moist and fingers fidgeting, looking to Gilmore for yet another intervention with the college authorities, a stay of execution. Rooting fretfully in his satchel, he withdrew the letter informing him of his imminent departure and handed it shakily to Gilmore, who was already familiar with its wording, its regretful but firm tone. Their ensuing conversation was mercifully brief. Gilmore knew this day would come, that following some brief but fruitless talk of appeals he'd end up dispatching the poor lad empty-handed.

'Try to think of this as a new beginning, Oliver ... an opportunity to consider a different career path for yourself.' Reddening, he found himself unable to look Prendergast in the eye as he said this, an ironic twist not lost on him. The relief he felt immediately after Prendergast's departure was quickly replaced with a profound sense of futility. He'd done all he could for this lad, given him a fair shake. Hadn't he?

Guilt pecked at him like a malign little bird for the rest of the afternoon, distracting him from getting any work done. His gaze finally turned to the framed family photograph on the shelf of his wife and boys staring back at him from Venice just three summers earlier.

'Give me a dig out here, Lizzie. What would you do?' But then he already knew what her answer would have been. She'd have quoted him some little Shakespearean wisdom about how *the quality of mercy is not strained ...*, as she nearly always did after patiently enduring one of his increasingly frequent rants about the sorry state of academia.

Leaving his office later that afternoon, he spotted the tattered novel still sitting on the edge of his desk, surprised not to have noticed it earlier and even more taken aback that Prendergast had abandoned it so casually. 'Probably expects me to read the damn thing,' he muttered, dropping it into his briefcase.

'Has the nurse left?' asked Gilmore, upon arriving home. His son Daniel was in the living room, thumbs flickering effortlessly over his mobile.

'An hour ago,' Daniel replied without looking up. 'She left you a note on the kitchen table, said to call her if there are any problems again tonight.'

'And Theo?'

'He's out in the garden with Mam,' Daniel said, still absorbed in the WhatsApp thread on his phone.

'Has he done any study today?' Gilmore asked.

'Yeah, right,' Daniel sniggered, shooting his father a look that said *What do you think?* 'The only thing that lad's studying is the back of his ball sack.'

'Ah, Danny! That's quite enough of that,' he sighed.

He walked through to the kitchen and sat wearily at the table, plopping his briefcase down on the floor beside him where it fell over, spilling out its contents. Frowning, he retrieved Prendergast's book and opened it, noting his name and address neatly written in the top right-hand corner of the inside front cover. Intrigued, he turned the book over to the publisher's blurb on the back, the corners of his mouth slowly lifting as he read: *House of Leaves ... Danielewski's cult novel concerning a house whose plain exterior belies a richly mysterious interior realm that constantly rearranges its rooms and hallways into ever more complex and unknowable dimensions.*

'Well now that sounds curiously like a metaphor for somebody I know,' he chuckled, shaking his head in wonderment. 'Clever little fecker!'

He had the uncanny feeling that Prendergast was sending him a message, giving him a sideways peek into the unusual geography of his mind, and in so doing deliberately prompting him to try looking at things differently.

At least that's what he *wanted* to believe.

Either way, he suspected he'd be reading for much of the weekend.

'Okay then, *O*,' he finally decided. 'Maybe you're not a completely lost cause. Perhaps part of the problem is me. I'll speak to the faculty on your behalf and we'll try a different approach. Probably come to nothing but sure we'll give it another lash and see where it takes us.'

Imbued with a renewed sense of usefulness, he felt his mood lift for the first time that day. He rose then and went to the kitchen window to look out at Liz who was seated at the end of the back garden with their younger son. Stretched out on a blanket wearing his tie-dye t-shirt and sweatpants, not a care in the world, he was smiling up at her, their quirky little Theo, as soft and sweet as jam.

'That lad's away with the fairies,' he'd once said to her. 'He's got two gears – slow and stop.'

'He'll turn out fine, Alan. He might not be the standard model, but he's a good kid. And kind. That's the most important thing.'

'He hasn't an academic bone in his body. How in God's name is he ever supposed to make something of himself?'

'They all take a different path, love, you know that. Have a little faith in him and he'll shine, just you wait and see. Our Danny did.'

The evening sun glinted off the spokes of her wheelchair. Theo was now kneeling before her holding the straw from a teacup to her lips so that she could take a sip, her once graceful limbs now clumsy and withered. He then used a napkin to gently dab away the tiny rivulet of milky tea that ran down from the corner of his mother's wordless mouth. Gilmore melted at the tenderness of the exchange.

'No, not quite the standard model, my love,' he whispered. 'But kind. So very kind.'

A Comparative Anatomy of Angels

Anouk Kupiec

i didn't actually mean to cause the end of the world this time, if that counts for anything.

after the first few times, i've almost gotten used to it – the quiet cities, the gleaming cars parked in neat lines along the roads, the empty prams in front of abandoned houses – but the drones passing by overhead with loud mechanical whirring sounds are starting to freak me out more than i'd like to admit.

Someone has been following you. You've seen her a few times now, creeping across rooftops and through hallways, always disappearing out of sight as soon as you try to get closer. She's not supposed to be here – no one is, Frankfurt was on fire when you left it and you still remember the morning you woke up in Naples to find the city empty – but after a while, the feather-light footsteps circling you when you're trying to sleep at night behind barricaded doors and shuttered windows seem almost comforting.

When you wake up to find her in your room, staring at an angel mural plastered across the front of the building on the other side of the street, you know you're in deep shit.

i fucking knew i shouldn't have gone back to berlin.

1.

Ava, as she introduces herself, speaks with a nasal accent that sounds like it's stuck somewhere halfway between French and Polish, and can't be much older than fifteen or sixteen, although her shaved-off hair makes her look a bit older. 'I wasn't there when it happened,' Ava says one evening, sounding strangely ashamed. She doesn't say where she was instead, but you suppose it doesn't really matter. You weren't really there, either.

Your Polish is terrible, and she seems to prefer not talking at all, so you end up communicating in a strange mishmash of languages and gestures, if at all.

'I still don't understand why you're following me,' you say one evening, when the constant silence is starting to get on your nerves again.

She looks at the window, then lowers the blinds. 'You have a problem, yes?', she asks quietly, voice rough from disuse. 'You go to city, and the city goes ...' Her hand flaps in a vague imitation of an explosion.

it started in utrecht, of all places – i'd spent every summer there since i was six years old, and one morning i woke up to see the word KINDEREN[1] *plastered across the walls of my hotel and found the city deadly silent.*

A drone whirrs by outside, the sound eerily loud. Ava hesitates, indecisive, flicking her fingers in a nervous gesture. 'I have ... how you say ... similar problem, yes? Every city I go to, everybody's gone.' She pauses. 'But ... someone comes. Follows. After a while.'

in gdańsk, it had started a day later than usual – i'd learned not to get my hopes up since i left most of the netherlands flooded, but still, it had been disappointing to wake up and find the hostel completely cleared out.

She perks up. 'But I have theory. For you, it happens after you arrive somewhere, for me, it's before. Maybe together, we can ... what, cancel each other out?'

Out of all the things you imagined you'd be doing in a postapocalyptic scenario, babysitting a fifteen-year-old who heats up pelmeni in tea kettles (you knew your tea tasted funny this morning) was not among them, but it probably doesn't make a difference anymore.

'Fine. Pack your stuff, we're leaving tomorrow.'

2.

That night, you climb up on the roof of the highest building you can find. Sitting on the ledge, you spot the murals for the first time: slogans in languages you don't understand (*je ne parle pas français*[2] comes to mind unbidden and plays on repeat in your brain for a week) and haphazardly drawn angelic silhouettes that you initially mistake for Nirvana logos. You snap a few photographs on the brick phone you've picked up in one of the empty malls back in Frankfurt, and when you look at them more closely a few days later, you notice that the smiling faces on the billboards advertising toothpaste and luxury cruises and makeup have all been blacked out. You leave Berlin the next day, but the blacked-out faces follow you all the way across the border.

3.

Ava seems nervous about leaving the city but doesn't explain why, and stops sleeping at night, instead curling up by the windows to stare at the sky with her strange, washed-out hazel eyes. The angel murals keep popping up, even in the smallest villages or at rest stops – as do the painted-over words and slogans on the walls of larger houses and village squares – but you don't get any closer to figuring out what happened, or what they mean.

You've just passed into Hungary – 'No, still Slovakia,' Ava says with absolute conviction, but neither of you can be bothered to check – when you see the elderly couple. You try to approach them – other people! Maybe the world hasn't come to an end yet! – but Ava holds you back with a death grip on your upper arm.

'No,' she hisses, panicked. 'Can't talk. *Proszę cię,*[3] don't go.'

The man and the woman haven't reacted to your struggle, although they are close enough to hear you.

'What's the matter with you?' you ask, jerking back your arm. 'Maybe they can help us.'

Ava lets go of you. 'No one home,' she snaps, frustration clear in her voice. No one there. I've seen it ... early ... no, before.'

Carefully, you take a few steps closer and the two of them turn their heads towards you in unison, following your steps with colourless eyes that flicker like TV static.

Something cold creeps up your spine and you reach out for Ava blindly, strangely relieved when she grabs your hand and pulls you back.

'Told you so,' she doesn't say, but it's clear from her look.

4.

The further you go, the more people you come across, all of them silently staring at you with those unnerving, flickering eyes. You haven't suggested talking to them again, but you've asked Ava if there's something you can do to help them. There's something unreadable in her expression when she leans against the wall furthest from the windows – she tends to avoid these nowadays, you've noticed. 'I've tried before, on my way from the north. They don't talk. And when the ...' She trails off, muttering something in Polish that you don't understand. 'The flying things,' she declares triumphantly. 'When they show up, these ... guys with the TV eyes disappear.'

That's probably the most you've ever heard her say in one go, and it takes you a moment to properly understand what she said. 'What flying things? Does it have anything to do with these angel murals?'

'Mural?' Ava asks. 'Like painting?'

You show her one of the pictures on your phone and she shrugs. 'Maybe the whirring things are angels,' she says, sounding for all the world like she's both serious and completely unimpressed. 'I'm not going to find out.'

You agree to keep moving, and you make it all the way to some city – empty and clean, like all the others – before the sun sets. Like in all the other cities, the drones keep whirring on overhead, just out of sight.

Ava doesn't comment on it when you double-check the locks on the doors to the gym you're sleeping in, and she doesn't comment on it when you hand her the kitchen knife you picked up in a restaurant a few days ago.

After a while, her soft, even breaths and the metallic whirring outside are the only noises you can hear, and you feel sleep tugging at you with heavy fingers. Careful not to startle Ava, you curl up between her and the door, your own knife placed underneath the dusty book you're using as a pillow (*A Comparative Anatomy of Angels: A Complete Guide for the Educated Cryptoanthropologist*, written in 1825), and close your eyes.

That night you dream of TV static for the first time.

[1] *kinderen* (Dutch): children
[2] *Je ne parle pas français* (French): 'I don't speak French', title of a popular German pop song.
[3] *Proszę cię* (Polish): Please.

Luas

Naoise Deeney

You will bump into me, I imagine. I will drop my wallet and a family photo will fall out. You will pick it up and hand it over. You will take out your wallet. You will show me the family photo you keep with you. A bond will be had, owing to this shared habit. 'Where are you going?' you'll have to ask me.

As luck would have it, same direction as you.

'What are your plans?'

I will have none of my own.

'Come with me.'

Whatever you say. I have nothing else to do.

I will follow you through city streets. You will lead me to a tattoo parlour. You will have your septum pierced and afterwards, we will go clubbing. On the dancefloor, you will twirl and clap your hands. You will also wave your arm around, like a lasso. What you will not do is get low, low, low, low, low, low, low to 50 Cent, because that's what everyone does. And you're not quite like anyone else.

'I really enjoyed tonight.'

'Yah. Me too.'

'Will we meet again?'

'We will meet whenever.'

Whenever will be Wednesday. I will get to know more about you. You will lead me into little shops and we will look at little ornaments. You will have the symbol of Aum tattooed onto your bicep and you will wear flares, instead of jeans. As a joke, you will ask a stranger for directions to a hemp farm. Any hemp farm. They will frown at you. You will glance back at me and smile, with cheek. I will smile too, because I am also good fun.

A week in, what you must do, as a means of self-expression, is buy a bucket hat from a charity shop. I have never been to a charity shop before but we will go together. You will tell me about how convenient it is before going inside, and once inside, I will experience how convenient it is. 'This is my first time,' I might say, and to that, you have free reign over your response.

A fortnight in, we will sit indoors and watch the weather. If it rains outside, we will step outside. If it rains elsewhere in the country, we will travel to the rain. And once rained upon, you will shake your wet hair and dance. You will shuffle in a puddle. I will clap, because I like you and the energy you bring. You're my kind of girl, I'll think, but you will never know these secrets.

I will then become depressed, for some significant reason I will refuse to talk about, because of how significant it is. I will sit on a bench by the canal, or by a pier, or somewhere in the vicinity of water. You will hold me and I will not hold you. I will keep my arms by my sides. I will do this because of solitary feelings. My actions will be an expression of my feelings, you see. You will massage my back, or caress my hair, and say, 'I understand', or something similar, but I will stare straight ahead and think to myself, *She couldn't possibly understand.*

Later that night, in a hotel room, I will break down and you will cuddle me. 'I don't deserve you,' I will say, because of how considerate and compassionate you are. You won't argue with me. You will just shush me and hold. I will hold you back. A process of healing will take place and for a time, things will be good. We will be happy together. And then you will change. I will not know why. An unspeakable misery will have entered your life and I will be tasked with breaking through.

At first, I will be very nosy. You'll have to forgive me. I am not as patient as you are. I can still be naive. But I will recognise that meddling is not what's needed. I will visit you on the porch while you sit on your swing chair, staring straight ahead. Or I will stand by your side while you feed the birds in your dressing gown. I will hand you a cup of tea and not say a word. I will simply be there.

I will hold strong until the night of your breakdown, when you will reveal all. I will be mad at those that caused your pain. I will be motivated to punch a wall. This will be an expression of my unbearable anger, you see. I will march back and forth in a rage and this will stir you from the swing seat. You will follow me, back and forth, and try to calm me. 'I'll kill them!' I'll say. Or, 'Those bastards!' Or, 'Motherfuckers!'

'Let it be,' you will say, and I will fall down into tears. So poignant, you are. We will hold each other and cry it out. We will heal and enter a new chapter.

Six months in, we will attend a wedding. We will drink and when it is time to dance, I will stand by and watch, because I am not much of a dancer. You will dance with another man and I will wait at the bar, quietly working on myself, reminding myself that there is nothing promiscuous about this, that dancing is just something you like to do. I will handle it very well, you will observe. When you come to the bar for a drink, you will see that I am in great humour, that there is nothing the matter with me. And while you dance, you will see me talking to other women, because conversation is how I get my kicks. You will handle it very well, I will observe. It will not offend you in the slightest, owing to our deep understanding of one another and our commitment to personal liberty. It can therefore be forgotten about. It wouldn't even be worth mentioning. On the walk back to the room, I will be enthusiastic and indifferent. You will be the same, I hope.

We will make a good team, but we will have our drawbacks. We will become dependent on cannabis together. For a time, this will be the gel of our relationship. 'When will we smoke?' will be the unifying question. It will be our token of attraction. We will become familiar with each other only when we're high. Sobriety will become awkward. But I will bring the issue to our attention in some moment of importance. The context I can't quite make out now. Maybe there will be a haze of smoke between us. Just know that I will criticise our activities with great emotion. I will call for change. You will be reluctant at first, but I will be patient, having learned from you. I will give you room, so that you can come to your senses, independently. And once you do, we will work together to pull ourselves out of this rut. Our cooperation will be unmatched.

We will learn to love the old attractions. We will check where it is raining and we will go there. I will clap and watch you shake your hair in the rain, and dance in a puddle. You will ask a stranger a silly question and turn to me and smile, cheekily. You will stand at a railing on a clifftop, before a pleasant view, and I will approach you from behind and perform the following manoeuvre: my hands running down your arms, gripping your hands, my body pressing into yours, you pressing back, my face flanking your head, the wind whipping me with your hair. I will smell your hair then, I think. I predict a strong urge to smell your hair. If I do not want to fulfil the urge, if I do not want smell to pollute the memory, which is already visually rich, I will let you know, so that maybe you could not use shampoo that morning. Or maybe you could use shampoo that isn't scented. We will feel warm and complete then, I trust. And then it will all be over. This moment, as with all moments, will need its replacement.

A suggested replacement would be bumper carting. We will drive around in separate carts and you will smash into a parent and child. The child will cry. You will apologise to the parent and glance at me. I will be laughing. You will hide your eyes with embarrassment and smile from the thrill of it. It will be a poignant smile. A smile I wish could last forever, knowing well that it cannot. This will bring about a short-lived sadness. Short-lived, because we will soon be onto the next.

We will buy cotton candy and wear it as hair. Or we will win a large teddy bear by shooting targets. Or we will go to Starbucks and have Willy and Fanny written on the cups. Or we will go to a niche café and drink homemade coffee. Or we will foreplay in the cinema. Or we will do the Viking tour. Or we will go to Venice. Or we will lie in bed and listen to 'Aline'. Or we will read *Mein Kampf*. Or we will take LSD and paint. Or we will scuba dive on mescalin. Or we will skydive. Or we will wrestle in a kids' pool. Or we will hold hands at a relative's funeral. Or we will go vegan. Or we will try the carnivore diet. Or we will lie on train tracks to feel alive. Or we will get drunk in the morning. Or we will get matching tattoos. Or we will sell nudes. Or we will join a protest we disagree with. Or we will travel the world. Or we will watch an execution. Or we will get pregnant, accidentally. Yes, we will get pregnant. 'I don't know what to do,' you will say.

'I'm with you no matter what.'

Over the following days, little will be said. We will meditate and keep cool, so that the answer might rise above its alternatives with patience. We will have changed for one another, so much so that the air about us will feel different. A week later, you will approach me while I'm drinking coffee and reading the paper. I will be wearing glasses, for some reason yet to be discovered. 'I want to keep it,' you will say. I will jump up and hug you, probably. To be honest, I don't what know I'll do exactly, but rest assured, it'll be something nice.

Initially, there will be an outpour of support, from friends and family. As the months roll on, there will be less. Our circles will grow smaller, but we will support each other. The air about us will become dense with trust. We will hold our own, find our way, and at last, you will bear me a child. I will cut the cord and hold it in my arms. It will be crying. Then it will stop crying. If it is possible, it will open its eyes, so that I can see that they are purple. I will look into your purple eyes, teary with content, and thank you, for having made me the happiest chap on the whole fucking –

Doors open. Girl on Luas steps out.

The Crannóg Questionnaire

Ivy Bannister

How would you introduce yourself as a writer to those who may not know you?

Born west of Kerry, Dublin's been my home since the 1970s. As a writer I've tinkered for years with every genre except film, producing a slow – and not necessarily steady – flow of work over time. Three books have appeared, one each of stories, poetry and memoir; and stories, poems, plays and essays have been published, broadcast or performed 'here, there and everywhere' (as The Beatles might say), picking up the occasional award along the way.

When did you start writing?

When I was 13. Everyone was reading Daphne du Maurier's *Rebecca*, so I started it, but was bored stiff. Then I turned a page, and suddenly a few thrilling words shattered my complacency. The idea that words could be so powerful took me over. I entered my secondary school writing contest and won, in spite of being the youngest competitor. Naturally I was impressed with myself and foresaw a glorious future in literature. Alas, I wrote precious little else until I was thirty.

Do you have a writing routine ?

I rise with the birds and exercise vigorously to the music of the dawn chorus. After a high-protein breakfast, I race to my desk for eight hours of fluid, flawless creation. Haha, fooled you! But yes, routine is everything, and my one rule is to write every day. I try to start early, but life interferes. On a bad day, the writing gets pushed into crannies of snatched time, but something always gets done. I review the day's output, either in the afternoon, or in bed for a fifteen-minute edit, which eases my way the next morning. Apparently my brain figures things out while I sleep.

When you write, do you picture somehow a potential audience or do you just write?

As a 19-year-old student who needed money, I wrote a few stories that could be sold to *Woman's Way*. In those pre-decimalisation days, *Woman's Way* paid in guineas, which added a gleaming, welcome shilling to every pound. Happily, nowadays financial needs are less pressing, so I write what I want, but always with an eye on where it will be sent. Publication is a joy: it's affirmation, my drug of choice. As a writer, I'm driven to make each piece as good as it can be: stretching my boundaries, rewriting, rewriting more, or, 'Try again, fail again, fail better'. With each project, I need to feel (if only for an instant) that I'm creating something special, and maybe even a work of genius. It's this outrageous optimism that keeps my fingers poised on the keyboard, or gripped around the black, fine-liner pens that I favour. If I don't believe in what I'm writing, how could anyone else?

Some writers describe themselves as planners, while others plunge right in to the writing. Would you consider yourself a planner or a plunger?

Both. My head is a jumble of stuff, but occasionally one subject crowds the others out. So I sit at my computer and let rip; everything tumbles out. This mind-dumping can be exhilarating. A one-page poem often starts with four pages of incoherent chaos. Before printing, I'll type in bold at the top what (I think) the poem is about, where it's going, and how I'm going to get it there. That's the plan, which I look at first thing each day, always trying to tighten it up ... Writing fiction or plays is the same, but on a larger scale.

Tell us a bit about your non-literary work experience please.

My first paid employment was removing dandelions from a lawn: you had to dig deep for the taproots. Next, it was two summers in the box office of a summer stock theatre in Connecticut. For 8 weeks (from the comfort of the box office), I studied the Herculean endeavours of the small staff, who ran one show, while building the set for next week's. This taught me about people and how things work. At night, I watched the plays, repeated viewings that drummed narrative and characterisation into my subconscious ... My third job was three plummy summers in the typing pool at *The New Yorker*. Sometimes, there was nothing to do except read the magazine, or mooch around the hallways, hoping to rub shoulders with the various luminaries who drifted about. But the work could be intense too, if there was an Edmund Wilson manuscript, written in blunt pencil on yellow foolscap in the tiny crabbed handwriting of an elderly man. There were arrows, inserts and excisions everywhere; the job was to make a clean copy, using manual typewriters and two-person proofreading. And if Mr. Wilson misspelled something, we had to too, exactly as he wrote it ... These three jobs provided a sound foundation for a writer.

What do you like to read in your free time?

Half my reading is memoir, biography or history. At the moment it's *Walt Whitman's America*, by David S. Reynolds. Books with pictures are important too: fine art books that seduce the eye and inspire dreams. And children's books. There's nothing better than a well-written children's book to get me up to speed on an uncongenial subject (physics, for example, that's very uncongenial). There are must-read novels too, the recent Booker winner, *Orbital*, and buzzy new Irish writing like Colin Barrett's *Wild Houses*. And it's essential to have a poet on the go: at the moment it's Whitman (no surprise), but by the time you read this, I hope it'll be Michael Longley.

What one book do you wish you had written and why?

One book? No way, not with my incurable case of Writer's Envy. First there's J.G. Farrell's *Troubles*, a novel that cemented my love affair with Ireland, a book that grows with rereading. Once upon a time, my difficult mother advised me to write books that are 'short and fun to read', which I ignored, like everything else she said. But oh, how I wish I had written some of Barbara Comyns' magnificent short books, sunny and dark at once, funny and heart-breaking, books like *Our Spoons Came From Woolworths* or *The Juniper Tree*. And how about *King Lear* or *Heartbreak House*? or, even better, both. And the wonderful poems of Elizabeth Bishop or Derek Mahon ... I could go on ...

Do you think writers have a social role to play in society or is their role solely artistic?

It's a gift to occupy space in this precious, fragile world of ours. Like most people who've been as lucky as me, I've tried to give back in various ways. With specific regard to writing, I've mentored on a voluntary basis, authors whose work interests me, long hours with wonderful individuals with whom it's been a privilege to work.

Tell us something about your latest publication, please.

I've had a couple of personal essays published recently (in *Look, It's a Woman Writer* and *Well, You Don't Look It*). There are two more memory-driven essays, completed, but homeless for the moment (Maeve Binchy regarded rejection as a temporary inconvenience, and claims to have kept stamped, preaddressed envelopes by her door, so that when a piece came back, she could immediately forward it to the next editor). In writing my essays, I've discovered how one memory wakes up others, and at present, my essay project appears to be taking on a life of its own.

Can writing be taught?

Of course it can, it's a craft. One good way is to teach yourself by ... eh ... writing. Barbara Taylor Bradford famously advised against starting a novel until you've lived a bit. In the meantime, she said, write a thousand words a day. Malcolm Gladwell equates success with 10,000 hours of effort. So, write, write, write. And while writing, dip into other things that will help you, for example Stephen King's inestimable *On Writing*. And reread a favourite book ten times, working out how the author has done it. There's one thing about writing, however, that can't be taught, what the director and writer Conall Morrison calls the 'sanctuary lamp'. I know what he means, but can't define it exactly. It's something to do with the magic and power behind really good work. It's spark, inspiration, the imprint of the soul. And not to worry if your soul is dark. There's always been a market for the dark stuff.

Have you given or attended creative writing workshops and if you have, share your experiences a bit, please?

Attending or giving – no matter which – I'm a creative writing workshop junkie. A year or so ago, I found myself in a one-day workshop intended for beginners. The person giving it turned out to be a young poet in love with poetry. He was fun, and there were a dozen unfamiliar faces to watch. I came away with a shiny new poem that I was glad to have written. Because writing is solitary, I need to get out and about with my eyes wide open ... The best workshop I ever took was decades ago with Frank McGuinness. Frank had a plan for every session, practical points he thought we should know. And he was awash with generosity of spirit. I'd go home, brimming with ideas, ready and able to write because of his enthusiasms. Which is not to say that you can't learn from a bad workshop as well. The worst I ever attended was given by a well-known playwright at Listowel Writers' Week. The night before, the hotel bar was busy. A lively young woman was chattering about how she'd been hitch-hiking, when the playwright whizzed right past her in his car without stopping. When the man himself appeared in the bar, the woman flew at him like a hawk. Soon, champagne was being drunk by the pair of them; and it didn't take much to see where things were heading. Next day in the classroom, the young woman pulled her chair forward, took out a peach, and sank her teeth into it! The playwright's hungover face was a book, riddled with humiliation and loathing, for himself as much as for her. The lesson here is that life's all around us. Plots, if you're looking, can be licked up off the footpath. As a facilitator myself, my goal's been to give the Frank McGuinness type of workshop, and not the latter!

Finally, what question do you wish that someone would ask about your writing, and how would you answer it?

Here's my question: Do you keep a journal?

Of course I do. My journal is my life's blood as a writer. It's always to hand, on the desk, beside the bed, or in my handbag. It gets written in constantly: notes, descriptions, feelings, phrases, ideas, banalities. Sometimes the writing is mindless; rarely, it's muscular. There's glued-in stuff too: emails, photos, poems I fancy, cut-out images, scraps of giftwrap and the occasional ivy leaf, especially if I'm abroad. When other people take out their phones, I take out my journal. I'll sketch in it, or scribble, trying to catch the moment or a face, a scrap of dialogue or a dazzling phrase. A heap of these motley journals have accumulated, millions of forgotten words, all catching dust in an over-sized bookcase. They're the best insurance that any writer can have: I'll never run out of subject matter.

Artist's Statement

Cover image: *Growth* by Blake McGrane-Corrigan

Blake McGrane-Corrigan recently completed his PhD in Mathematical Biology at Maynooth University and is now a researcher in Ecological Modelling at University College Dublin.

In his spare time he draws and writes poetry. One of his drawings has previously been published in *Ghost City Review*.

The drawing featured on the cover of this issue, in ink and pencil, reflects on the idea of rewilding, our often-overlooked dependence on nature, and the silence we face following its destruction.

Biographical Details

Fatema Alzari is a Bahraini writer and illustrator. Her work has been published in *Sekka Magazine, Orangepeel Magazine, Bahr Magazine, Liverpool Art Festival* amongst other print publications.

Catherine Balaq has been published in numerous anthologies and journals. Her work has been shortlisted for the Bridport Prize and nominated for the Pushcart and Forward Prize. Her poetry play *Fuck the Moon* was commissioned by Paper Nations and short-listed for the Bristol Old Vic Open Sessions 2019. She is working on her first novel, *Halloweg*. She is co-editor of Black Cat Press. Her debut poetry collection *animaginary* was published in July 2023 with Black Cat Press and is nominated for the Seamus Heaney Prize for first collection and the Pen Heaney Prize. Her second poetry collection *Deathless* was published by Verve in 2024.

Elizabeth Barton's debut poetry pamphlet, *If Grief were a Bird*, was published by Agenda Editions in 2022. She was a prizewinner in the Shelley Memorial Poetry Competition 2023 and was Highly Commended in the Ver Poets Open Competition 2024. Her poetry has been published in journals such as *Agenda, Acumen, Mslexia, The High Window* and the podcast *Poetry Worth Hearing*. She is Stanza rep for Mole Valley Poets and editor of their anthology.

Bern Butler's poetry has been published in *Ropes Anthology, North West Words, Abridged, The Ireland Chair of Poetry, Dodging Rain, Ink, Sweat and Tears, The Madrigal, Skylight 47, The High Window, Ragaire*. She was a featured reader at Cúirt's New Writing Showcase 2021. She has an MA in Writing from NUIG.

Finola Cahill won the 2023 Waterford Poetry prize and the 2024 Single Poem Award at Writers' Week, and has been shortlisted widely, including for the Fish, Bridport, and Sappho poetry prizes.

Áine Rose Connell has received bursaries from the Arts Council, artsandhealth.ie, and Creative Ireland for her socially-engaged practice, combining literary craft with participatory art. Her writing has been listed in the Seán Dunne Poetry Competition (2024) and the Cheltenham International Poetry Competition (2023). Her writing has appeared in *Drawn to the Light Press*, *Trasna* and *A New Ulster*. She was selected for Poetry Ireland's Introduction Series (2024).

Phil Cummins is an Irish writer of fiction and creative non-fiction with work published in *Crannóg, Fictive Dream, Sans. PRESS, bioStories, Solstice* and elsewhere. His work has been placed in several competitions including the Fish Memoir Prize, Wild Atlantic Writing Awards, Fish Short Story Prize and Write by the Sea. Instagram: @profphilcummins

Martina Dalton's publication credits include: *The Irish Times*, the *Irish Independent*, *Poetry Ireland Review*, *The Stinging Fly* and *Rattle*. Anthologies include: *The Stony Thursday Book*, *Washing Windows Too*, III, and IV (Arlen House), *Local Wonders*, and *Romance Options* (Dedalus Press). She has been shortlisted for the Julian Lennon Prize for Poetry, won third prize in the Red Line

Poetry Competition, and second prize in the Waterford Poetry Prize. In 2022 her poem 'Wedding Dress' won Poem of the Year at the An Post Irish Book Awards. She is a Words Ireland mentee.

Rebecca D'Arcy has published poetry in *The Blue Nib* and *The Storms* issues 2 and 4. Her short stories have been published in *Tir na nÓg* and *The Martello.*

Patrick Deeley is a poet, memoirist and children's writer. *Keepsake*, his tenth collection of verse, was published by Dedalus Press in 2024.

Naoise Deeney is a graduate of English Literature with Creative Writing from UCD whose fiction has appeared in *New Word Order* magazine and *Caveat Lector.*

Annie Deppe is the author of three books of poems, most recently *Night Collage* (Arlen House, 2021).

Theodore Deppe is the author of eight books of poems, most recently *Impossible Blackbird* (Arlen House, 2024). His poem *Lullaby Before Leaving* was one of the four shortlisted for the Poem of the Year at the Irish Book Awards, 2023. He has received a Pushcart Prize and published in *Crannóg, Poetry, Poetry Ireland Review, The Stinging Fly, Cyphers, The Kenyon Review, Ploughshares, The Forward Book of Poems*, and elsewhere.

Mauk Donnabhain is a queer, working-class writer. His short story *Drowndead* was placed 2nd in the Flash 500 Short Story award in 2024, and he was shortlisted for the Stockholm Writers' Festival's First 5 Pages award in 2023. He has had work shortlisted for The Plaza Prize: Sudden Fiction (2023), and the Colm Tóibín International Short Story award (2020) and longlisted for the Minds Shine Bright competition (2023). He has had work published in *Crannóg, The Honest Ulsterman, Profiles Literary Journal, Trasna, The Galway Review, The Belfast Review*, and others.

Ger Duffy's poems have appeared in *PNR, Poetry Ireland Review, Banshee, Southword, Under the Radar, Verve EcoPoetry Collection, The Ekphrastic Review, The Sailor Review, The Stony Thursday Book.* In 2024 she won the Desmond O'Grady Award and The Redline Poetry Competition, her pamphlets were commended in the International Pamphlet & Poetry Award and shortlisted for the Patrick Kavanagh Award. She was awarded an Agility Award by the Arts Council of Ireland.

Barbara Dunne is a writer and visual artist. She was a finalist in the Desmond O'Grady International Poetry competition. She has been published in *The Storms Journal, New Word Order, Drawn to the Light Press, HOWL: New Irish Writing, Crannóg, Skylight 47* and in other journals and online. She is working on her debut poetry collection.

Katherine Duffy's publications include the pamphlet *Talking the Owl Away* (Templar Poetry, 2018), and two previous collections with Dedalus Press. Recent work has appeared in *Poetry Ireland Review, The Interpreter's House*, and *Drawn to the Light*.

Annie Egan works as a researcher specialising in the rights of the child.

Billy Fenton writes fiction and poetry. His poetry has been widely published including in *The Rialto, Irish Times, Cyphers, Banshee, Poetry Ireland Review, The North, Acumen, Orbis, Crannóg, Abridged*, and many others.

Tracy Gaughan's chapbook *What it Costs* is published by Southword Editions. Individual poems have featured widely in magazines and anthologies. Her short story collection *Weather Readings* is published by BelleClare Press.

Elizabeth Gibson's poems have appeared in *Abridged, Banshee, Butcher's Dog, Dust, Fourteen Poems, The Honest Ulsterman, HOWL, Lighthouse, Magma, The Storms*, and *Under the Radar*. Her debut collection, *A love the weight of an animal*, will be published by Confingo in 2025. https://elizabeth-gibson.com. Instagram: @Grizonne.

Ruth Gilchrist is a poet and flash fiction writer. Her writing has appeared in various journals including *Dreich, Under the Radar, SouthLight*. Her first solo pamphlet, *Bird Brained, a Bird Count in Poems*, is published by Black Agnes Press. She is working towards her first full collection.

Kevin Graham's first collection, *The Lookout Post*, was published by Gallery Press in 2023. It was shortlisted for the John Pollard Foundation International Poetry Award and won the Southword Debut Poetry Collection Award. A second collection is forthcoming.

Linda Ibbotson is a poet, artist and photographer and has been published widely, including in *The Irish Times, Irish Examiner, California Quarterly, Limelight, Boyne Berries, Washing Windows Too*.

Maria Isakova Bennett, a teacher, writer and artist, works for charities and creates the hand-stitched poetry journal *Coast to Coast to Coast*. Her awards include The Peggy Poole from The Poetry Society, and a Northern Writers' Award. She has created collaborative work with over 100 poets from the UK, Ireland, and France. She worked with poet John Glenday to create *mira* (an exhibition and journal, 2020). She has had five pamphlets of poetry published, the latest, *an o an x*, in 2023 by Hazel Press.

Ellen Kelly's short stories have been broadcast on RTÉ Radio 1 and published in *The Irish Times* and previously in *Crannóg*. She has been shortlisted for various awards including the Francis MacManus Short Story Award, the Hennessy Literary Awards and the SBP/Penguin Ireland Award. She was nominated for the Pushcart Prize in 2021. Her debut novel, *Her Last Words*, came out to critical acclaim in 2022.

Anouk Kupiec is a writer and multimedia artist. Her illustrations have been featured in the literary journal *Leopardskin &amp, Limes* and several of her poems have been presented at the Federal Agency for Political Education in Mainz as part of the German-Ukrainian art project Paperovyj Tyhr in September 2023.

Jennifer McMahon was the overall winner of the 2024 All-Ireland Scholarships Creative Writing Award (Public), a winner of the Irish Writers Centre Novel Fair (2023), was a second-place winner of the Oxford Prize (winter 2023), was shortlisted for Short Story of the Year at the Irish Book Awards (2023), the Bridport Short Story Prize and many other notable awards, was longlisted for the Bath Short Story Award, and was nominated for Best Of The Net in 2024. Her work appears in *Crannóg, HOWL, Irish Independent (New Irish Writing), The Galway Review, the Oxford Prize Anthology (2022 and 2023), Fractured Lit, Heimat Review (issues 2 and 6), Empyrean, Books Ireland, Loft Books (issues IV and V), the Retreat West 'Swan Song' Anthology, the Cowboy Jamboree 'Motel' anthology, Frazzled Lit, and The Irish Writers Handbook* (2024 and 2025 editions). She is the co-editor-in-chief of *Frazzled Lit*, and is represented by Brian Langan at Storyline Literary Agency.

Winifred McNulty's poems have been published in *Poetry Ireland Review, Banshee, Mslexia, Cyphers, Under the Radar, The North* and other magazines. She has won the Boyle, iYeats and Westport poetry prizes. She has read her work on RTÉ and is currently working on an Arts Council funded Artist in the Community project.

Ray Malone's work has been published in numerous journals in the US, UK and Ireland including in *Poetry Ireland Review, The Stinging Fly, Southword* and *Crannóg*. He is working on a series of projects exploring the lyric potential of minimal forms based on various musical and/or literary models.

Wendy Mooney's work has previously been published in *Poetry Ireland Review, Cyphers, Crannóg, Windows Publications: Authors & Artists, New Irish Writing* and many other journals.

Patrick Moran has published four collections of poetry: *The Stubble Fields* (Dedalus Press, 2001), *Green* (Salmon, 2008), *Bearings* (Salmon, 2015), and *Reckonings* (Salmon, 2019). A fifth collection, *Birding*, is forthcoming. His poems have appeared widely in Irish outlets, and also in the UK. He is represented in Windharp, an anthology of poems written since 1916 by Irish poets. His work has featured on RTÉ radio's *Sunday Miscellany.*

Eamon O'Riordan was shortlisted for the 2023 Bridport Short Story Prize and has had work published previously in *The Honest Ulsterman* and *The Antigonish Review.* He is completing a short story collection.

Ciarán O'Rourke's second collection, *Phantom Gang*, was longlisted for the Dylan Thomas Prize in 2023. His third collection is forthcoming from The Irish Pages Press.

Arlene Pattison facilitates creative writing workshops for marginalised groups and is currently working towards an MA in Creative Writing and a first poetry collection.

Ana Reisens' poems have been published in *The Threepenny Review*, *The Four Faced Liar*, and *Channel*, among others. She has been nominated for a Pushcart Prize and Best of the Net.

Bill Richardson's poems have been published in numerous magazines, including *Amethyst Review*, *The Stony Thursday Book*, *Orbis*, *The Orchards*, *The High Window* and *Skylight 47*, as well as in collections such as the *Fish Anthology 2020*. He is Emeritus Professor in Spanish at the University of Galway, Ireland.

Moya Roddy is the author of two collections of stories, *Other People* (Wordsonthestreet)) and *Fire in my Head*. Her stories have been published in *Crannóg*, *Penguin*, *Michael Joseph*, *Serpents Tail*, *The Irish Times*, *Quiddity* (USA) and many others. She has also published two novels, *The Long Way Home* (Attic Press) and *A Wiser Girl* (Wordsonthestreet) and two poetry collections, *Out of the Ordinary* (Salmon Poetry) and *The Dark Art of Darning* (Salmon Poetry).

John Saul's fiction was published in the Dalkey Archive's Best European Fiction 2018, representing fiction from England. His fourth collection of short fiction was published in 2025 (confingopublishing.uk). His work has been published recently in *The Stinging Fly* and in *Best British Short Stories 2023*. He is a member of the European Literature Network. www.johnsaul.co.uk

Gerard Smyth is a poet, critic and journalist whose work has appeared widely in journals in Ireland, Britain and the United States as well as in translation. Recent publications include *The Sundays of Eternity* (Dedalus Press, Dublin, 2020) and *The Haunted Radio* (Brighthorse Editions, St Paul, Minnesota, 2024). He is a member of Aosdána. www.gerardsmyth.com

Laura Theis' work appears in *Poetry*, *Oxford Poetry*, *Magma*, *Rattle*, *Aesthetica*, *iamb*, etc. Her Elgin-Award-nominated debut *how to extricate yourself* (2020), an Oxford Poetry Library Book-of-the-Month, won the Brian Dempsey Memorial Pamphlet Prize. *A Spotter's Guide To Invisible Things* (2023) received the Live Canon Collection Prize and the Society of Authors' Arthur-Welton-Award. Other accolades include the Alpine Fellowship Writing Prize, AM Heath Prize, Poets & Players Prize, Oxford Brookes Poetry Prize as well as a Forward Prize nomination. Her new collection from Broken Sleep Books and her children's debut *Poems from a Witch's Pocket* (Emma Press) are both forthcoming in 2025.

Dolores Walshe was awarded two Arts Council Bursaries, the Berlin Writing Prize, Bryan MacMahon Short Story Award, O.Z. Whitehead/Pen Playwriting Award and has twice been a prizewinner in RTÉ's Francis MacManus Award. Her plays have been staged in Dublin and Manchester and published by Syracuse University Press, New York, and by Carysfort Press, Dublin. A novel and a short story collection were published by Wolfhound Press. Her stories and poetry have been broadcast on Irish national radio and published in various anthologies and literary journals including *Sand Journal*, *Southword Literary Journal*, *Crannóg Literary Magazine*, *Visual Verse Anthology*, *Fish Anthology*, *The Irish Times*, *Poets Meet Politics Anthology* and *The Arrow Journal*.

Janice Warman is an award-winning writer of YA fiction, non-fiction and poetry. Her work has been published in the UK and South Africa, in her women's literary survival guide, *The Hey Nonny Handbook* (Harriman House), in *Ballet*, a poetic and photographic tribute to her mother (Susakpress/Spiralbound) and in English textbooks in South Africa. She is past winner of the Kent & Sussex Poetry Society Folio Competition. Her journalism career spans *The Guardian*, *The Observer*, the *Financial Times* and BBC Radio 4. She has taught creative writing as a volunteer at Share Community for disabled adults for eight years.